Crystal Clear
Communication

To Stuart —
Welcome to ANP Banking!
Best wishes,
Kris Cole
May '98

The Competitive Edge Management Series is a joint publishing venture between the Australian Institute of Management NSW Training Centre Ltd and Prentice Hall Australia Pty Ltd. Books published in the Series will provide today's practical managers with the skills and insights they need to achieve a competitive edge in the marketplace. The Series will enable Australian authors and their scholarship to be published to appropriate markets by using the resources of these two organisations. Enquiries about books in this Series or information regarding the submission of manuscripts should be directed to either partners in this venture.

Crystal Clear Communication

Skills for Understanding and Being Understood

Kris Cole
Bax Associates Pty Ltd, Adelaide

PRENTICE HALL

New York   London   Toronto   Sydney   Tokyo   Singapore

Acquisitions Editor: Pat Evans
Production Editor: Fiona Marcar
Cartoonist: Peter Broelman
Typeset by Keyboard Wizards, Allambie Heights, NSW

Printed in Australia by Star Printery, Erskineville, NSW

4 5 97 96

ISBN 0 7248 0185 5

**National Library of Australia
Cataloguing-in-Publication Data**

Cole, Kris.
   Crystal clear communication.

   Bibliography.
   Includes index.
   ISBN 0 7248 0185 5.

   1. Interpersonal communication. 2. Nonverbal
   communication I. Title.

153.5

Prentice Hall, Inc., *Englewood Cliffs, New Jersey*
Prentice Hall Canada, Inc., *Toronto*
Prentice Hall Hispanoamericana, SA, *Mexico*
Prentice Hall of India Private Ltd, *New Delhi*
Prentice Hall International, Inc., *London*
Prentice Hall of Japan, Inc., *Tokyo*
Prentice Hall of Southeast Asia Pty Ltd, *Singapore*
Editora Prentice Hall do Brasil Ltda, *Rio de Janeiro*

PRENTICE HALL

A division of Simon & Schuster

Foreword

We are living in times of huge change—change to the way we live, work and think—much of which has been brought about by unprecedented access to information. As we know, knowledge is power. The important question for all of us becomes how to gain and process information so that it enables us to order and become effective and powerful in our private and corporate worlds. We can achieve this goal by gaining knowledge through effective communication with other people.

We need skills that our parents and schools didn't teach us so that we can be sufficiently aware of ourselves and others, and able to give, receive and evaluate information.

These skills are the essence of communication and Kris Cole covers a huge range of contemporary thinking in a way that is crystal clear. Her excellent writing style and presentation of text, and the brilliant illustrations (many of which completely bypass the need for verbal interpretation), communicate directly from mind to mind.

Congratulations on the publication of an important tool for use in an age where information is abundant and communication is scarce.

Warren Mills
Organisation Development Manager
Beaurepaires

Contents

Part III Gathering good information
Learning how things are from the other person's point of view 137

Part IV Watch that body language!
Improving communication through body language 175

Part V Put it in writing
Writing for clarity and persuasion 213

Further reading 237

Index 239

*I*ntroduction

Communication is a central part of our lives. Verbal or written, symbolic, nonverbal, intentional or accidental, active or passive, communication is essential to almost everything we do. In fact, most of us spend between 50 per cent and 75 per cent of our working days communicating in writing, face-to-face, or over the telephone. Given that 80 per cent of our communication is spoken, *what* we say and *how* we say it is critical to our success.

It is through, and as a result of, communicating with others that we can accomplish many of our aims and ambitions, that we can make significant progress and achieve success with projects and our day-to-day work.

Fortunately, effective communication is a skill which can be developed. It requires conscientious and thoughtful practice and the application of straightforward, although not necessarily simple, techniques. Through practice, our skills will develop and our understanding—of communication, the communication process, ourselves, and others—will deepen.

Acknowledgments

I have many people to thank:

Thank you to all the authors of interpersonal skills and self-development books and seminars whose ideas I've borrowed, adapted or built on.

Thank you, Alan Hyde, for teaching me about fact, fantasy and folklore.

Thank you, Graham Andrewartha, for your insights on the Six Basics of Communication.

Thank you, Jeff McComas, for the statistical information on the voice, and for teaching me about the importance of our 'vocal instrument'.

Thank you, Janet Chin, for helping me understand Asian body language. Thank you to the people at Tandanya for your information on Australian Aboriginal people's body language.

Thank you, Ilse Jamonts, for unlocking the door to effective communication.

Thank you to the people who have attended workshops I've led for your thought-provoking questions, for offering your ideas, opinions, experience and insights, and for helping me think things through and reach and test conclusions.

Thank you, Mom, for teaching me. And thank you, Don, for your substance, spirit and strength.

PART I

The basics

Understanding and taking charge of your communications

Everything we do is communication

1

Every day, in many ways, we communicate. We communicate our thoughts, our feelings, our desires. We communicate whether, and how much, we like and respect someone. We communicate happiness, uncertainty, delight, misery. Simple or complex, intentional or unintentional, planned or 'ad hoc', active or passive, communication is one of our key tools for achieving results, satisfying our needs, and fulfilling our ambitions. Whether we do it well or poorly, communication forms a major part of each of our days.

WE COMMUNICATE TO:

complain

gain credibility be polite warn

improve self-esteem command, direct give help

help each other praise fool around

motivate cheat deceive form friendships

survive get help barter, deal socialise

purchase something get information entertain get the job done

tell, inform learn make money gain respect

greet make arrangements express ourselves

abuse reassure give advice sell

pass the time

Our communication skills reflect our ability and confidence; they highlight our talents and accomplishments and affect how much appreciation and respect we receive from others. These skills have a direct bearing on our promotions, pay rises, responsibilities, and career path. They directly affect the level of support and help we receive from others, and dictate our ability to have our ideas accepted and implemented.

Why do we communicate?

Studies tell us that 70 per cent of mistakes in the workplace are a direct result of poor communication. Yet avoiding mistakes is only one of the many reasons people communicate. As the graphic on the previous page indicates, there are many other reasons that people communicate.

Factors cited by managers as creating communication difficulties:

- lack of information or knowledge
- not explaining priorities properly
- not listening
- not understanding fully and failing to ask questions
- mind made up, preconceived ideas
- not understanding others' needs
- not thinking it through clearly, jumping to conclusions
- losing patience, allowing discussion to become heated
- short of time
- bad mood
- failure to explore alternatives.

If these difficulties are not recognised and dealt with, it stands to reason that the effectiveness of communication will be severely reduced.

Communication failures can cause:

- loss of business
- loss of goodwill
- reduced company image
- loss of sleep
- loss of enthusiasm
- mistakes, inefficiencies
- decreased productivity
- drop in self-esteem and confidence.

- frustration, hostility
- unhappy staff
- lowered morale
- loss of creativity
- loss of team spirit
- high-employee turnover
- absenteeism

These are results we don't want and can't afford!

Communication then, has a profound impact on our daily lives and relationships, and more important, on the *quality* of our daily lives and relationships.

So here are the six basics of communication.

COMMUNICATION BASIC

1   **Everything we do is communication.**

People are full of verbal and non-verbal, intentional and unintentional messages. The words we say are only the tip of the iceberg—they make up between 7 and 24 per cent of the message, depending on the situation.

When we choose what to wear in the morning, we choose something that communicates a message about our self-image and self-esteem. The cars we drive, the houses in which we live, the clothing and accessories we choose—these all communicate how we feel about ourselves and how we wish to be treated by others.

When we place personal items on our desk, we communicate something else about ourselves: what we believe is of importance and worth.

Whenever we move or change our posture, seating position, or facial expression, we express something about our attitudes and feelings. The words we choose to use and omit and the strength and energy with which we say them also tell a story.

These communications may be unconsciously sent and received, but sent and received they are, nonetheless.

COMMUNICATION BASIC

2

The way the message is delivered always affects the way the message is received.

Messages are made up of far more than the words we use. The volume and tone of voice we use, the degree of eye contact we make, our stance, the tilt of our heads—all these help the receiver to interpret our words and take meaning from them.

So, although we may not consciously think about every aspect of the way we deliver a message, the way the message is delivered is *always* an important factor in the way it is received.

COMMUNICATION BASIC

3

The real communication is the message received, not the message intended.

It is alarmingly easy for a message to be received in a way that is far different than the one we intended. And it is fair to say that the *real* communication is the message that is received by others—regardless of our intentions. Good intentions don't necessarily make for good communications.

COMMUNICATION BASIC

4

The way we begin our message often determines the outcome of the communication.

At one time or another we have all experienced the sensation of being rubbed the wrong way, when someone first speaks. If we're not careful, our first few words can cause people to tune out, to get their backs up, to become defensive—to reject our message. Part of the success of any communication, then, depends on the way we choose to begin it.

DID YOU HEAR THE ONE ABOUT THE DRUNK, BALD, ONE-EYED BIKIE?...

**COMMUNICATION
BASIC
5**

Communication is a two-way
street—we have to give as
well as gather.

There are two vital elements in successful communication: **giving good information** and **gathering good
information**.

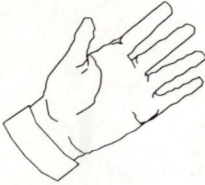

On the one hand, we want to state our own
point of view clearly, fairly, and persuasively.
But if this is all we do, we haven't got
communication—we've got a harangue or a
diatribe.

So, on the other hand, we need to hear the
other person's point of view clearly if the
communication is to succeed.

**COMMUNICATION
BASIC
6**

Communication is a dance.

While it includes giving and gathering good information,
communication is much more than just giving and receiving
a message. It is a *reciprocal* process. It is something
that happens between or among people. We do it *together*.

For instance, this book *itself* isn't the communication.
The communication lies in the meanings *you*, the reader,
take from it. You are part of its communication. If no-

one reads this book and therefore takes no meaning from it, no communication will take place. All we would have is symbols on paper.

Communication is a dance. It happens *between* people. We communicate *with* others; we don't talk *at* them. Pet budgies and parrots talk *at* us, not *with* us!

Even if we deliver the same message several times over to different people, separately, or in groups, it will be different. We will be different (we might have learnt something from earlier deliveries; we may say it differently because we're thinking it through differently; we may be in a different frame of mind). The group we are delivering it to will be different from the last group. The forces between the communicators will be different. And so we will dance the communication differently.

The receivers of our message will be different, too. Different people will hear the same message differently because they are different people with different back-

Communication is a dance. It is different each time.

Have you ever discussed something with someone and found that you were able to clarify and develop your ideas as you spoke? You may have even discussed the same thing with someone else with no clarification or development of your ideas. The difference is in the *process*—what is going on between you. This is the *dance* of communication. Like the old saying goes:

IT TAKES TWO TO TANGO

grounds, experiences, and belief systems. And so the communication dance will be different.

These, then, are our six basic building blocks of communication. The rest of this book explores how to make the most of them.

What happens between two people trying to communicate with each other? What thoughts run through your mind each time you communicate with a stranger; a friend; a co-worker; a senior executive? When you meet someone for the first time? When you disagree with what they say? What assumptions do you make? What expectations do you hold? How does your past experience affect what you hear?

How you say it is what counts

Your voice is an instrument

Words are important. Yet words are only a tiny fraction of the message that is received. *How* you say those words—your **tone** of voice (harsh, soft, neutral, rising, falling), **pitch** and **volume** (high, low, loud, soft, or modulated), **speed** (fast, slow, or medium), and the **emphasis** you place on those words, are all important. They not only affect the message that is ultimately received, but also, first impressions. In fact, 38 per cent of a listener's first impression of us will be based on how we sound.

11

Emphasise for clarity

Most people are partly aware, at least, of the emphasis placed on words. There are seven words in the sentence to the left; read the sentence seven times, aloud or to yourself, emphasising each of the seven words in turn.

I never said he lied to her.

You have seen that changing the emphasis on just one word can totally alter the meaning of a message. Often, we emphasise words without realising we're doing so, unconsciously 'giving the game away' or 'showing our hand'.

At least twice a day, or more if you can, remind yourself to check your communications. The more often you do this, the more habitual it will become. Eventually you will check your communications automatically, without even being conscious of doing so.

Checking our communications, really listening to what we're saying and how we're saying it, being conscious of the effect our message is having on others, will help us choose the most effective emphasis as well as voice tone, pitch, volume, and speed.

Use tone, pitch, volume, and speed to best effect

Some voices sing; others are rich; some are warm and friendly; others condescending; still others are flat and monotonal. Our voice tone is the quality of the sound of our voice, its expressiveness or colour. Through inflection, it expresses moods, emotions, and differences in meaning. Pitch is the intensity, volume, and variety with which we speak and whether we speak with 'high notes', 'low notes', or an interesting mixture. Speed and pitch make powerful combinations: some people's voices ooze like molasses; others twitter breathlessly and quickly; some people force their words out like bullets from an automatic rifle. How quickly or slowly, how high pitched or low we speak also affects the way others perceive us and receive our messages.

We are not born with any particular way of speaking. Rather, we develop characteristic voice tones, pitches, volumes, and speeds through experience and habit, without conscious thought or volition. This is a pity because the human voice is a rich and variable instrument, and with practice it can enhance and reinforce our messages to ensure that the message received is close to the message intended.

Your voice will have more volume and richness if it comes from deep in the diaphragm rather than high in the throat.

How quickly do you speak? Do your words tumble together making it difficult to follow them and to form a word-picture, or do you hesitate so much that people become impatient or lose the thread of what you're saying?

> Breathe deeply, and relax your neck muscles and vocal cords. Practise reading aloud, into a tape-recorder if you can, until you achieve a quality, pitch, variety, and clarity you are satisfied with.

Speed should be related to:

- **The subject**. For example, how complex is it? With complex subjects we need to give the listener more time to assimilate what we're saying.
- **The listener**. How quickly does he or she speak? Try and moderate your speed to be more aligned with the listener's rate of speaking (see also Chapters 15 and 25).

> Try to get 70 per cent falling inflections at the end of sentences. Newsreaders are trained to do this because the presentation sounds more authoritative.

Spoken Australian

Despite the fact that the human voice can cover two octaves, Australians tend to speak in a **monotone**, with little movement or range in sound. We also tend to speak **too fast**—over 165 words per minute. Most people don't think in words, but rather, create pictures with them; 165 words per minute is too fast for 'picture-making' and leads to many listeners giving up. We tend to **emphasise** 'if', 'and', 'to', 'but', 'at', 'of'. Why? These are not what is important and stressing them leaves the key words unidentified. We keep our **lips too close together** . . . we **lack expressiveness** . . . we have **rising inflections** at the end of sentences and word groups which make us sound as if we're seeking approval. In short, there is a lot of room for improvement in our spoken communication.

What you *intend* to say, then, can be totally undermined or powerfully strengthened by how you say it. Think about your delivery and practise improving it.

Navigating the obstacle course: identifying and overcoming communication filters, barriers and incompatibilities

3

Communicating effectively is much like negotiating an obstacle course. There are obstacles within ourselves, called communication **filters**, which serve to screen information and messages, limiting our understanding and thus the effectiveness of our communication. There are **barriers** in the external environment which can frustrate communication. And there are **incompatibilities** between ourselves and the other communicator which can easily lead to misunderstandings and even conflict.

FIXED IDEAS

PREJUDICE

ASSUMPTIONS

STEREOTYPING

CHAPTER 3

Be aware of communication filters

Fact number 1

Our parents and other influential people combine with our life experiences to develop within us certain beliefs, 'mind sets', 'mental sets', paradigms, ways of looking at the world.

+

Fact number 2

The brain strives for order and predictability.

=

Fact number 3

The brain, in its attempts to create order, automatically interprets our life experiences according to our paradigms. So, as we live, our paradigms and mind sets tend to be continually reinforced.

X

Fact number 4

To avoid what psychologists call 'cognitive dissonance', we tend to ignore information that is clearly contrary to our beliefs and paradigms.

=

Very strong communication filters.

The need for order and predictability, the tendency to see what we 'expect' to see and to ignore contradictory information, and the sheer power of habitual thinking, blend to form potent and rigid communication filters.

These filters are like well-worn ruts or pathways in our brain. Because our brains work so rapidly, these filters snap into operation in a fraction of an instant. As most of our filters or paradigms are unconscious, or below our level of awareness, we are not aware of them, and so we tend not to examine them to see whether they are realistic, up-to-date, helpful, or even valid.

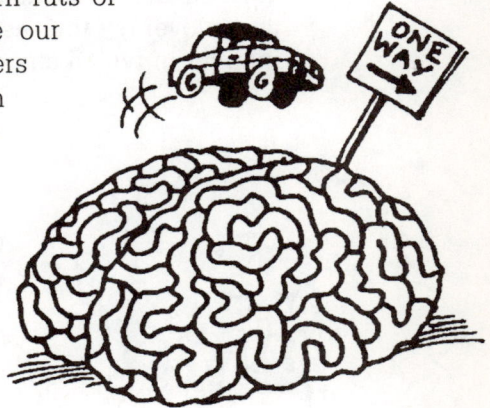

Of course, some of these mind sets are worthwhile and stop us having to reinvent the wheel. For example, 'I should be pleasant and respectful to the boss' and, 'You get out only what you put in', are probably two useful beliefs that a lot of managers have.

Other mind sets, however, are less useful and less valid, and hinder communication between people. Ideas about how people 'should' behave, assumptions, mind sets, and paradigms, all need to be checked against reality from time to time.

Whether or not they are valid or helpful, our mind sets, paradigms, and fixed ideas are easily confirmed and strengthened. For example, if we have a mind map that says 'I'm shy and most people don't like me much', we readily accept signals from others that we can interpret as 'They're not interested in what I have to say', and 'He dislikes me', and ignore any signals of friendliness or desire to listen to us.

So we receive and interpret only signals of dislike and disinterest, reinforcing that particular belief. Moreover, because we subconsciously want to be assured that our mind sets are correct, our behaviour to others is based on the 'fact' that we 'know' they don't like us, and we also behave in a way that *invites* them not to.

On top of this, the other person also has his or her own mind set. Imagine that the older character in the cartoon below assumes that all young people are lazy and slovenly; this assumption will directly affect the manner in which she communicates with young people.

The young man, too, will have his own assumptions and mindsets. Suppose he believes all old people are mean and nasty?

We now have two people, talking not to each other, but to their **images** of each other. We can gauge how ineffective communication is likely to be!

Once aware of these paradigms and prejudices you can often update or adjust them so that they become more useful and realistic. If this is not possible, acknowledging a prejudice and putting it to one side is the best course of action.

When you get the sense that you are not talking to a real person but at your image of him or her, stop and think: what mind set is influencing me? What mental image, prejudice, or stereotype am I the victim of? What assumptions have I made that might be invalid? Examine your assumptions and preconceptions and redraft them from the logic and experience you've gained.

Bill was a middle-level manager who prided himself on being fair and open-minded. He believed he had uncovered and dealt with many of his communication filters. One early filter he recognised was that he felt drawn towards and comfortable with people with European accents. He worked out that this was because his grandparents had European accents and he was close to them as he grew up; he also decided that there was nothing harmful with this particular prejudice, so while he remained aware of it, he accepted it.

Recently, his mother was remarried, to a man with a European accent. Unfortunately, Bill strongly disliked this man and noticed that now, instead of feeling positive towards people with European accents, he felt quite negative towards them. His attempts to redraft this reversal of his mind map failed, so he decided to acknowledge it and put it to one side whenever he needed to communicate with Europeans. Although it took effort, Bill believed that consciously working to ignore this prejudice was in his own, and everyone else's, best interests.

Apart from our paradigms, we all have a large collection of other types of filters which serve to obstruct the communication process.

Become conscious of the way you communicate with other people; identify which filters obstruct your communication; acknowledge these, and take steps to remove or reduce them.

Some common communication filters

- premature evaluation
- other things on your mind
- tendency to jump to conclusions
- prejudice
- your mind wanders easily
- inattention
- assumptions
- stereotyping

- stress
- poor listening skills
- short attention span
- hearing difficulties
- 'selective hearing' (hearing only what you want to hear)
- fixed ideas
- preconceptions
- preconceptions

Reduce communication barriers

Then there are barriers in the environment outside: noise, distractions, too many things happening at once, and so on. These barriers can make concentration difficult

SMITH AND I WERE WONDERIN' IF WE COULD GO AND FIND A QUIET PLACE FOR A NICE CHAT, SIR?

or cause us to hear only part of a message or a garbled message. They can make us uncomfortable or nervous, reducing our ability to think clearly and communicate well.

A willingness to block out noise and distractions and centre your attention solely on the other person is one good way to overcome such barriers. Move to a quieter place or one with fewer distractions, or reschedule your meeting to a more convenient time. Ask not to be interrupted. Focus your attention by listening carefully and mentally outlining the key points of what is being said.

Overcome incompatibilities

Sometimes we are different from, or incompatible with, the other person in some way that makes it difficult, awkward, or uncomfortable for us to communicate. Age, gender and race differences, differences in background, education, personalities, value systems and life styles fit into this category. Such incompatibilities can invoke communication filters such as stereotypes, prejudices, premature evaluation, and even stress, often without us realising it.

If our view of the world is totally different from another person's, it can be very difficult to 'talk the same language'.

Sometimes we express a message poorly; perhaps one of us is hard of hearing or doesn't speak clearly; perhaps one of us is trying to make too many points at once and succeeds only in being confusing.

Recognising such blocks will help us to overcome them and achieve successful communication. We can ask questions, revise our message, speak more slowly or loudly—whatever it takes to gain understanding.

In Chapter 5 we'll discuss the meaning and importance of empathy and how this can help overcome basic differences and incompatibilities.

The main thing to remember about the obstacle course is that it is always there, for everyone. We each have our own unique set of obstacles. Awareness of them and the desire to overcome them, combined with patience and understanding for the other person's obstacles, go a long way towards making our communication more effective.

Behaviour breeds behaviour

4

'Treat others as you would have them treat you'

'You reap what you sow'

'Behaviour breeds behaviour'

These are phrases many of us are familiar with.
What do they really mean?

'The Law of Psychological Reciprocity' has a nice ring
to it for those who like impressive-sounding jargon.
What does it really mean?

Each means the same thing:

Behaviour breeds behaviour

In summary, we know that people tend to respond to
us as we treat them.

We reap what we sow:

Be rude and people generally will
be rude to you.

Be polite and people generally will
be polite to you.

Be considerate and people generally
will be considerate to you.

Be respectful and people generally
will be respectful to you.

Most of us have experienced the delight of unexpectedly excellent service and the 'glow' that resulted; we may even have been a little 'extra pleasant' to others as a result. Unfortunately, many of us have perhaps experienced the opposite: discourteous service which made us more short-tempered than usual and perhaps made us give as good as we were given. Others influence us—someone else's behaviour is breeding our behaviour.

The opposite also occurs: have you ever influenced someone who was, initially, unco-operative or unhelpful to smile and become friendly, just by smiling and being friendly to them? This happens all the time. It can be seen in restaurants, car parks, shops, and offices, every single day if you're on the lookout. This is because people have a natural tendency to respond in kind to the treatment they receive.

That's the Law of Psychological Reciprocity: 'If you're nice to me, I'll be nice to you; and if you're not, I'll give as good as I get'. This is how behaviour breeds behaviour.

Knowing this, you can take charge of much of the communications you enter into. What 'tone' do you want the conversation to take—relaxed and informal? By being relaxed and informal, the other person will tend to follow your lead. Polite and courteous? By being polite and courteous to others you will help them to be polite and courteous to you. Co-operative and frank? By being co-operative and frank you set the examples you want.

So all we have to do is decide how we want others to treat us. We then treat others that way, and Bingo! Actually, it isn't *always* that simple, but it's a very good, general rule of thumb. And it works far more often than not.

So, you can use your behaviour to influence others' behaviour. How much do others influence your behaviour?

Showing respect is one of the best ways to earn respect.

Use the Law of Psychological Reciprocity to direct communications and influence their results. You will reap whatever you sow.

You can choose your behaviour

If someone is rude to us, we have choices. Two of these choices are: to be rude back, or to be polite to try to influence them to be polite to us. In any communication we have options and each of these options has predictable results because we reap what we sow. And we can choose what we sow.

People are not born nasty, rude, or insolent, polite, friendly or helpful. How we treat others mainly depends on three things: how they treat us (behaviour breeds behaviour; Locus of Control (which gives us choice and which we'll examine below); and our mind sets (which we discussed in the last chapter. As we saw, we can bring many of these into consciousness, examine them, and change or update any that need it: *they're not fixed)*.

The fact that we can choose our behaviour is good news because it means that when something goes wrong, we can choose how we will respond to it. We don't have to unthinkingly react to it.

Locus of Control or pulling your own strings

'He makes me mad' is a phrase we have all heard. Is this possible—that someone else can force us to be angry? Or do we have more say in the matter? Let's examine the Law of Psychological Reciprocity more closely. We know that we can influence the other person's behaviour by our own. Does this work in reverse: can others influence our behaviour by theirs? Must we respond to others as they treat us?

Korri's weather

It had been an unusually rainy year. Korri Koala sat high up in her tree, very glum. 'I'm so *tired* of being damp. I'm so *tired* of the smell of dripping eucalyptus. I miss all the visitors pointing and "Oohing" and "Aahing."

Her friend Gum Nut ambled across to cheer her up. 'Struth, Korri, I don't know what's the matter with you. Only two seasons ago you were complaining that the visitors kept you awake! We've got plenty of lush growth here to eat and there's a lovely gentle breeze to rock us to sleep. Sure it's wet up here, but you don't need to let it get you down! You're bigger than a bit of rain!'

To some people, it doesn't matter whether it's rainy or sunny—they carry their own weather with them. It's more than just 'looking on the bright side' or 'positive mental attitude'. It's about Locus of Control: who 'pulls your strings'. You can control your own thoughts and behaviour, or you can let someone else do it.

People who carry their own weather with them don't need sun-shine to be happy—they carry their sun with them. They don't need to receive excellent service to get into a good mood, and poor service doesn't put them in a bad mood. Their Locus of Control is internal.

They're the people who breed courtesy in the discourteous; pleasantness in the unpleasant; helpfulness in the rude.

Others give away their Locus of Control; they allow other people to control their behaviour and determine whether they'll be happy or sad, pleasant or unpleasant, respectful or rude. These people have given up their freedom of choice. Their Locus of Control is external.

We'll talk about the concept of Self-Talk in Chapter 21. For now we can say:

> Listen to the silent messages you give yourself because they will give you a clue to your mind sets and whether your Locus of Control is internal or external.

So, others can influence our behaviour with theirs only if we allow them to. If we want to retain control and be able to choose our own behaviour, we will keep our Locus of Control internal.

If we accept that 'We can control our behaviour' by retaining our Locus of Control, we will never have to say: 'He makes me mad'. We will have a choice— whether to allow someone's behaviour to anger us or whether to acknowledge that their behaviour is annoying and carry on with our day unaffected. The latter is the more powerful position and one from which we can retain control over many of the communication situations, especially the difficult ones, in which we find ourselves.

> Because behaviour breeds behaviour and we can control our behaviour, we can, to a large measure, influence the result of any communication in which we engage. This means we can take charge of the communications we enter into. We can be proactive and get *more* of what we want— friendliness, courtesy, respect— *more often.*

Take charge of your communications!

Walk in another person's shoes, or you'll get nowhere 5

A world of difference:

Apathy

Empathy

Sympathy

There's a world of difference between these three words.

Apathy

Apathy is 'I couldn't care less!' This is the kiss of death to communication. We can't communicate very long or very well with someone who doesn't care about us or what we have to say.

Sympathy

Sympathy isn't much better. It involves feeling such a close affinity with someone that whatever affects one similarly affects the other. In most communication situations, this is far more than is necessary or even desirable.

Empathy

Empathy is quite different. It involves being able to see a situation from the other person's point of view. It doesn't necessarily mean you have to agree with it—in fact, you might totally disagree and still be able to understand it from the other person's perspective.

Empathy is about bringing us closer together so that we can understand and take into account the other person's point of view when we communicate with them. This helps us communicate in a way that will decrease any resistance or defensiveness in the other person and help them to hear more readily what we have to say.

How do we get closer together?

Lou was one of the company's most enthusiastic salespeople. He felt terrific when he made a sale and felt quite despondent when he lost one.

It seemed to Lou that lately, a lot of sales were being lost on price. He was convinced that if his manager would only give him the authority to drop prices, he could win many more sales.

When Lou went to his boss with this request, she said quite firmly: 'Lou, I realise how important sales are to you. I fully understand your wish to be able to drop prices further and I can see that you believe it would increase your sales. Sales are important to the company, too, and so are maintaining price levels. Let's see what we can do to win more of those sales by raising our level of support and service so that we don't have to drop our prices'.

Lou's boss *empathised* with him: while she didn't agree with him that there was merit in lowering prices, she was able to understand his point of view.

Contrast this with *apathy*—how well would Lou and his boss be able to work together if she were totally indifferent to his desire to drop prices and win sales?

Or what would happen if Lou's boss *sympathised* with him—felt as bad about losing sales as he did and let him drop prices, despite the company's policy? She wouldn't be able to function in her job effectively!

I CAN FULLY UNDERSTAND YOUR POINT OF VIEW...

Seek first to understand and appreciate
the other person's point of view

Understand the other person's frame of reference

Our Frame of Reference is made up of our background
and past experiences, what we value as important, our
beliefs, paradigms, and mind sets. Our personality types
and operating styles also form part of our Frame of
Reference (see Chapter 15). Some people, for example,
like detailed information while others are interested only

in 'the bottom line'. Some need friendly working relations with other people in order to work well while other people focus on 'getting the job done most efficiently'. Some value timeliness while others believe that what counts is doing a good job, no matter how long it takes. Different things are important to different people.

The more we can understand another's Frame of Reference—where they're 'coming from' and what is important to them—the easier it is to communicate with them. If we know what is important to them, we can structure our information to meet their needs. If we have an understanding of some of their background and past experiences, we can provide information in a way they can relate to and understand. We will be able to see things from their point of view. In short, the closer we can bring our Frames of Reference, the more able we will be to 'speak the same language' and present our message to gain the best results.

For successful communication we need to overlap our Frames of Reference—the way we see the world—as much as we can with the other person's. Because we have not had the same experiences as anyone else, a full or complete overlap is impossible. Sometimes, though we are so similar to another person in terms of upbringing, age, life experiences, and so on, that our Frames of Reference naturally overlap and we have an automatic empathy with them.

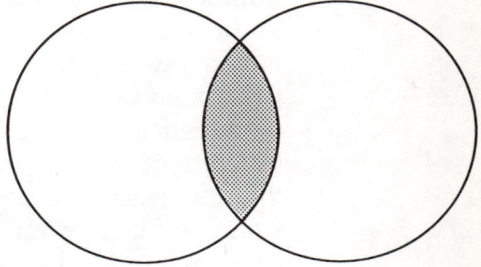

At other times, only very small overlaps are possible because of the many differences (see Chapter 3) which exist between two people; in such cases, our empathic skills are critical in our ability to communicate successfully. The more overlap we can achieve, whether through 'natural' empathy or consciously developed empathy, the better our communication will be.

This is the real meaning of empathy and this is why it is central to effective communication.

Effective communication involves us bringing our Frames of Reference closer together. We can then share the same, or at least similar, thoughts and ideas.

The communicator's pledge

Whether or not I agree or disagree with what you say, I will respect your right to say it and I will try to understand it from your point of view. This, in turn, helps me to communicate my point of view to you more effectively.

Develop empathy

Empathy is a skill. Like any skill, it must be practised until it comes naturally to us.

Develop empathy by taking opportunities to step into another person's shoes; to see a situation from their point of view. This means exploring the situation with them and asking questions; checking your empathy by stating, in your own words, what you understand the other person's beliefs and position to be; and imagining aloud to them what it would be like to be in their position and feel the way they do.

Try this first with people you know and have a good relationship with. As your skills develop, gradually increase the difficulty by practising empathy with people who are progressively more different from yourself, and finally, with people whose ideas and opinions you find most difficult to understand.

Practice makes perfect!

Conflict recipe: look for the common ground and beware the loser

'You have to give and take.'

'It's important that everyone wins.'

'Listen to the other bloke and find out what he really wants.'

'Everyone needs to be satisfied.'

'People will get you back if you walk all over them.'

In their own way, each manager is really saying the same thing: 'No-one really wins an argument if someone loses'.

Differences of opinion, disagreements, discord, rivalry, disharmony, disputes—in short, conflict in various forms— are commonplace in organisations. Will we allow conflict to become a source of stress, long-term friction, drawn-out battles? Or will we deal with it openly and honestly and try to resolve it fairly and to everyone's satisfaction?

Bring problems and difficulties out into the open and discuss them

One of the most important communication skills that successful managers identify is conflict resolution skills, and in particular, the ability to deal with conflict and work together to resolve problems in a way that satisfies both or all parties as much as possible.

To do this, we have to bring any problems or difficulties out into the open. Only then can we properly explore and discuss them. Once we've found out what the *real* problem is, we will be in a position to work together to resolve it. This is far better than imposing our own solution on another person.

How do you respond if someone forces their solution on you? Do you respond with resentment, anger, resistance? Do you want some form of revenge? Will they have 'won a battle but not the war' as far as you're concerned? This is how most people respond when something is forced on them and their needs are ignored.

Imposing solutions on other people, unless it is absolutely necessary, is poor practice. If you do choose to do this, you should also be aware of the consequences: resentment, anger, resistance, revenge and so on.

Five approaches to conflict

Collaborative, win–win approach

Talking things over is important. It helps us find a mutually acceptable solution, one that both parties can live with and support. This is the **collaborative, win–win** approach. It is the approach to take when it is important that our own, as well as the other person's wishes and needs, are taken into account—we both win. The win–win approach leads you to a double win in another way: not only is it good for developing workable *solutions*, it is also great for improving *relationships*.

There are other approaches we can take:

Force

We can, as we've discussed, *force* our solution on the other person. We know what the result will be in terms of the relationship: hostility. Sometimes the issue may be so important, or it may be so important to you that you have your own way, that taking the wishes and needs of the other person into account is not feasible. This is a **win–lose** approach: I win, you lose. Beware: losers have a way of retaliating.

Avoid

Another approach is to *avoid* the problem. This is a **lose–lose** approach where neither person wins because the problem is set aside and not dealt with. Chances are it festers and worsens in the long run. The relationship suffers and no solution is reached. Avoidance means that the wishes and needs of neither party are treated as important. The solution is often left to fate or chance.

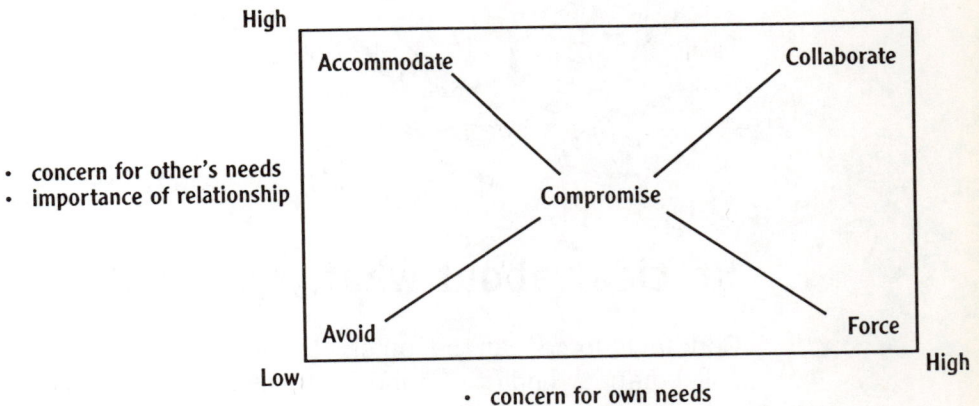

High

Accommodate　　　　　　　　　　　　Collaborate

- concern for other's needs
- importance of relationship　　　　　　Compromise

Avoid　　　　　　　　　　　　　　Force

Low　　　　　　　　　　　　　　　　　High
- concern for own needs

Accommodate

A fourth approach is to give in—to let the other person have their way. We pretend everything is fine and smooth things over. This is a **lose–win** approach because the other person's needs and wishes are taken into consideration, sometimes at the expense of our own. This makes sense if the issue is not important to us or if the relationship is more important than the issue. Sometimes it just makes sense to *accommodate* another, particularly if our wishes or needs are not infringed.

Compromise

The fifth and final way to approach conflict is to split the difference. Neither person has their wishes or needs met entirely but sometimes *compromise* is the best that can be done and is the approach that will least damage a relationship while still achieving a reasonably acceptable and workable solution. Neither person loses entirely, but neither is a winner.

Be clear about what you want

Certainly, force can be quick, but in the long term collaboration tends to be more satisfactory. People are more committed to the success of a plan which they have had a part in devising and which meets at least some of their needs. Revenge, resistance, or resentment are less likely. Relationships are likely to grow and strengthen.

When you are faced with a situation of conflicting wishes or solutions or when you identify a problem that must be resolved, be clear about what you want. What is more important to you—the **issue**, the **relationship**, or both? How hard are you willing to work so that both parties are satisfied?

Go for win–win

The concept of win–win is one of the key concepts in successful communication. How can we put it into practice? Here are some particular behaviours that successful managers have identified as helpful and unhelpful during difficult communication situations:

Helpful	Unhelpful
Focus on one thing at a time	Sticking to your own opinion
Be patient	Not prepared to admit the other has a point
Make it clear what is being discussed and why	Interrupting
Listen	Everyone talking at once
Respect the other's opinion	Unclear aims
Air grievances and problems	Shouting, losing temper
Want to reach agreement	Jumping to conclusions
Focus on what you agree on	Forcing 'solution' on the other
Focus on what you both want	Focusing on your own needs as a result

INGREDIENT NUMBER

1   **Mutual respect.**

If you respect yourself, you will naturally want to solve any problem or difficulty and make sure that your own wants and needs are met by its solution. If you respect the other person, you will also want to make sure that their wants and needs are met in any solution you both agree to. Mutual respect encourages you to go for a win–win solution.

INGREDIENT NUMBER *2*

Look for the common ground.

Rarely do two people have entirely opposing views with absolutely nothing in common. If you look hard enough, you are bound to find points of agreement on which to build.

INGREDIENT NUMBER *3*

Establish needs, wants, worries.

In any situation we have **needs** and **wants**—things that we *need* to happen and things that we would *like* to happen if we are to be satisfied. We also have **worries** or concerns—things we really *don't want* to see happen because they would, in some way, be detrimental to us or those we represent.

The other person also has needs, wants, and worries. Use your empathy to decide what these are; or if possible, ask.

When you write down your needs, wants, and worries and those of the other person, it usually becomes very clear that you share a number of them. Build on them; they are fertile common ground. A statement like: 'Lee, you and I both want X and I believe we're both concerned to make sure Y doesn't occur', can lead to fair-minded discussion and set you both to work on co-operatively resolving the conflict or solving the problem.

INGREDIENT NUMBER 4

Redefine the problem or point of disagreement if necessary.

If you absolutely cannot find anything to agree on, try redefining the problem or point of disagreement. A different set of terms, a different perspective, a different emphasis can sometimes break us out of a difficult situation.

INGREDIENT NUMBER 5

Focus on a result acceptable to all.

What do you both want? If you agree that you both want to increase profitable sales or to make the department a happier and safer place to work, it will be easier for you to find a solution. You will have a shared framework and goal to work towards.

INGREDIENT NUMBER 6

Give options and remain flexible.

Rarely is there only one solution to a problem. If you see the problem in terms of competing solutions, or if you see it in terms of 'only one possible solution—mine', it will be difficult, if not impossible, to resolve it to the satisfaction of all parties.

Have several alternatives in mind that would be acceptable to you; the more the better. Know also what would *not* be acceptable to you.

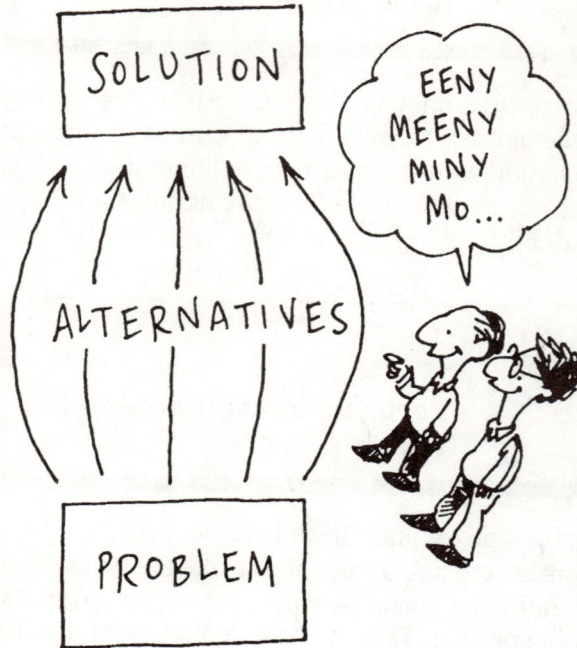

INGREDIENT NUMBER

7

Keep your mind open.

Rigid thinking, 'wearing blinkers', preconceived ideas—these destroy attempts at conflict resolution.

Your chances of success at solving a problem increase significantly the more you explore the problem itself and the more you search for alternative solutions. This opens your mind to a variety of options and allows you to explore these.

Your mind is like a parachute:

it only works when it's open.

**INGREDIENT
NUMBER
8**

Be positive, not negative.

Yes, behaviour breeds behaviour and negativity is catching. Negative statements like 'That will never work', 'We'll never get anywhere on this', or 'You're absolutely wrong', invite a negative spiral of counterattacks and arguments.

If you want to disagree, outline your reasons first, and finish up with something like: 'And that is why I don't agree with that way of looking at it'.

If you feel the discussion is going in circles and you feel like a break, say so directly! 'I think we've been over this ground a few times; perhaps it's time we had a break.'

A positive approach is catching. Clearly label all your positive and neutral statements: 'I agree and . . .', 'I'd like to ask a question', 'To summarise, then . . .'

INGREDIENT NUMBER

9

Work together to solve the problem.

Get the other person 'on side'—literally. It makes it very difficult to argue with someone sitting next to—not opposite—you. This allows a different attitude or mind set to surface: 'You and I are working together to solve or resolve a problem which we share'.

INGREDIENT NUMBER

10

Delete 'but' from your vocabulary.

But 'butts away' the other person's point. It negates what went before it. 'Yes, I take your point but . . .', 'The report was fine but . . .', 'You did a good job but . . .'

The word 'but' is responsible for a great deal of tension and disagreement. Delete it from your vocabulary! The same holds true for the word 'however'; this is just a longer version of the word 'but'.

Substitute 'but' and 'however' with 'and': 'I agree and . . .', 'I appreciate your viewpoint and . . .', 'I respect how strongly you feel about this and . . .'

INGREDIENT NUMBER 11

If your approach isn't working, change something.

'I've told you a million times!' Well, if it didn't work the first few hundred times, it probably won't work this time. Try something different!

If you are not happy with the results you're getting, change something: the environment (go somewhere different), your approach, your tactics, your communication style. It doesn't matter *what* you change, since what you're doing now isn't working, anyway. The keys are **empathy, Frames of Reference**, and **flexibility**.

INGREDIENT NUMBER 12

Take a deep breath.

Stress and tension inhibit thinking and stop the brain from working as efficiently as it can. You need your brainpower to communicate, to search for alternatives, to empathise. Taking a deep breath, or even two or three, can work wonders.

We've looked at 10 ingredients of the conflict recipe. Think them over carefully and imagine when or how you could put them to use in your day-to-day life. Be alert to how other successful communicators use them. Have a go at using them yourself—you'll be pleased with the results.

Communication is a two-way street—you have to get as well as give

As we saw in Chapters 1 and 3, communication is a process that takes place between people. All communication, even written communication, involves interaction between the communicators. External barriers

It takes two to tango

such as noise must be dealt with. Internal filters such as assumptions, previous experiences, self-image, expectations, and prejudice, are involved. Differences between the communicators, such as age, gender, race, educational backgrounds, and pastimes, flow between them. The dance of communication is a complex and often concealed one.

Two critical elements of the communication process which we can readily observe and influence are giving good information and gathering good information. We need to be able to give good information—to say how things are from our own point of view, and we need to be able to gather good information—to learn how things are from the other person's point of view. The cornerstone of these two elements is mutual respect.

There must be mutual respect

Two things are needed if we are to earn the respect of other people: first, we must respect ourselves; if we don't, no-one else is likely to; second, we must respect the other person; showing respect is a tried and tested way to earn it. Respect is a two-way street.

This is what mutual respect is about: respecting yourself and respecting the other person. Without it, successful communication cannot take place.

Give good information

You owe it to yourself, as well as the other person, to state clearly and calmly your point of view and all the facts as you understand them. That's *giving good information*.

Most of the time this depends on being able to give information in a way that the other person will be able to accept: by using their representational system (i.e. visual, auditory, kinaesthetic, or digital) in a style that will convey respect, encourage open, non-defensive listening, and be appropriate to their Frame of Reference.

Gather good information

To do this, you need to be able to *gather good information*. This primarily involves the skills of observation, listening, empathy, and asking useful questions. Attending to the other person's representational system and communication style, seeing things from their point of view (without necessarily agreeing), and finding out about the other person's wants and needs in the situation, will help you to give information in a way that it can be 'heard'. So giving good information and gathering good information are mutually dependent elements of effective communication.

We explore them in the next two parts of this book.

PART II

Giving good information

Saying how things are from your point of view

Avoid the 11 deadly sins of communication

8

Eleven deadly communication sins

Patronising

1. evaluating
2. consoling
3. 'playing psychologist' or labelling
4. making sarcastic remarks
5. excessive or inappropriate questioning.

Sending signals

6. commanding and 'railroading'
7. threatening
8. giving unsolicited advice.

Avoiding

9. being vague
10. withholding information
11. diverting.

Adapted from Robert Bolton, *People Skills*.

These behaviours are called 'deadly sins' because they quickly ruin any communication. They lead to guesswork, misunderstandings, irritation, frustration, and complete communication breakdowns.

Unfortunately, we see these sins being committed around us every day. This makes it easy for us to commit them too—after all, that's the way people talk to each other, right?

Yet this is not the way to communicate if you want your communication to be successful.

As you read about each 'sin', think about when you have heard it. How did you respond? Do you ever commit it yourself? When and with whom?

Patronising

Evaluating

When we pass a positive or a negative judgment on another, it implies that we think we are in some way 'better' than they are. This is especially so when we judge others in a general rather than specific way. 'You're a good worker', or 'You're hopeless' are both unhelpful because they are very general statements and will make the receiver feel as if they are being talked down to. So avoid general evaluations such as: 'You're being so inconsiderate!' or 'You'll need to be more committed if you're going to get anywhere'.

Be specific in your praise or criticisms. Never say what you Like or don't like without explaining why. Keep to facts rather than opinions and interpretations. Use neutral words and, at all times, convey your respect for the other person with your body language, tone of voice, and the words you choose to use.

Consoling

Another form of patronising is to reassure, sympathise with or console another person.

'You'll feel different tomorrow.'

'Don't worry, every cloud has a silver lining and I just know things will work out.'

'I feel so terrible for you.'

These are usually unhelpful comments because they tend to miss the mark. They also imply that we know better than the other person about their own situation; when you think about it, this form of communication is quite insulting.

Come from a position of mutual respect. Do not talk up or down to others. This helps you avoid being patronising. Try to stay away from clichés and empty reassurances.

Playing psychologist or labelling

In organisations or in our own social groups you have probably heard some of the following comments:

'You're just saying that because you've got a problem with authority.'

'You haven't fully understood.'

'Your problem is . . .'

'You're paranoid.'

'You're lazy.'

'You're not trying hard enough.'

Comments like these are examples of **labelling**—a way of communicating that once again puts us 'up' and the other person 'down'.

It is very dangerous to label people or their behaviour because we do not know whether we're right or wrong; and there's a high chance we'll be wrong. Yet we behave towards the other person as if we're right. This leads to all kinds of difficulties in communication.

Resist labelling people or their behaviour. If you want to change something they're saying or doing, describe clearly what you heard or saw, without interpretation or evaluation. Keep to the facts and, if you want, tell them what effect this behaviour is having on you. These are legitimate points of discussion. Amateur psychologists' interpretations are not legitimate.

Making sarcastic remarks

Although it is part of Australian culture in some circles, sarcasm is actually an aggressive put-down. Even friendly bantering can get out of hand and cause hard feelings. Sarcastic remarks inhibit open communication. Sarcasm, in fact, is in the same league as name-calling, ridiculing, and shaming; and it leads to the same results.

It's usually preferable to say what you mean, rather than veiling it in a sarcastic remark.

Excessive or inappropriate questioning

People don't like to be grilled or feel they're being examined or given the third degree. Do you? Asking one question after another, even if they are open questions requiring full answers, or asking a series of rapid-fire closed questions requiring a yes–no response or a short informative answer have that effect.

When you ask a question, make eye contact while the other is responding and show, by your body language, that you're listening—nod and grunt. Base your reply on something the other person has just said, or give a short summary. If you need to find out a lot of information you can then move on to your next question.

If you have many questions, it helps to ask permission: 'I'd like to ask you a few questions; do you mind?' Link your next question to the previous answer by briefly summarising. This will stop the 'staccato' or rapid-fire effect.

Sending signals

Commanding

Commanding is when you tell someone what to do in a way that leaves them no room to discuss, seek further information, disagree, or even agree. Your order makes the other person feel more like a machine than a person. Either an aggressive response or resentful submission will result, depending on your relative status.

The next time you're tempted to say 'You must . . .', or 'Stop it!', *you* stop! Look for a better way to send your message.

A more subtle form of commanding is known as 'railroading', where you politely, often through logical argument, make statements that assume the other person is in agreement, without giving them a genuine opportunity to air their views; by keeping the conversation moving along very rapidly, you 'browbeat' the other person into yielding to your point of view.

Use your empathy and phrase your message in a way that makes it easy for the other person to understand why you want something done or not done. Offer suggestions for improvement. As far as possible, focus on the *result* you want and let the other person decide what action should be taken.

If you find yourself leading a conversation quickly to the conclusion you want, ask yourself whether you could be 'railroading' or 'browbeating' the other person into submission. If so, is this what you want to do? Would it serve your purpose better and be better for the relationship to listen attentively to what they have to say?

Threatening

'If you don't . . .', or 'You'd better . . .'. Threats, either direct or more subtle, implied 'or else' messages, make people wary and widen the communication gap even further. Most people look for ways to defend themselves against threats. They look for ways *not* to 'obey'.

If there are good reasons why someone should or should not do something, explain them. Explain the consequences, too, if you want, accurately and fairly. Encourage rather than threaten.

Giving unsolicited advice

When phrases like: 'You should . . .', 'You ought to . . .', 'Have you tried . . .', and 'If you take my advice, you'll . . .' pop out of our mouths, we're in danger of sounding like we're moralising, preaching or lecturing.

If people want our advice or opinion, let them ask for it. Then they'll listen. If we force it upon them, they'll probably ignore us, making what we say just so much hot air.

If you *must* give some unsolicited advice, ask permission first: 'Would you mind if I make a suggestion?' or 'Would you be interested in hearing how I'd handle that?'

Avoiding

Being vague

If we don't come straight to the point people have to guess at what we really mean or want. As mental telepathy isn't all that common, they usually guess wrong!

Be specific! The keys are mutual respect, empathy, and speaking for yourself, or 'owning your messages'.

Being vague also involves not 'owning' your messages. 'Everyone knows . . .', or 'Most people agree . . .' are ways of *not* saying exactly what you think.

Withholding information

Some people release information only on a 'need-to-know' basis. This may have worked once, but today people need to know what's going on if they are to do their jobs properly and become successful and fully effective team members. Withholding information leads to game-playing and one-upmanship instead of successful communication.

If you have some information that you think will be helpful to someone, share it. You're likely to find out some interesting things in return, too.

Diverting

When the conversation becomes emotional or personal, or when another person begins to reveal something of their true self, people can feel uncomfortable and try to bring the conversation back to superficial matters. This leads to such behaviours as distracting the speaker, changing the subject or responding in clichés.

We are not compelled to have a 'deep and meaningful' conversation every time we talk to someone. On the other hand, conversations sometimes offer us more revealing, personal glimpses and to automatically discourage them is not always desirable. A team member or a co-worker might indicate they want or need to discuss something on a more personal level with us; successful communication is not achieved by shutting them out.

Centre your attention on the other person and use the active listening techniques discussed in Chapter 17.

Have you noticed the high 'you' component in these deadly communication sins? In Chapter 11 we'll talk more about why this obstructs communication.

If you catch yourself committing any of these deadly sins—STOP! Take a breath. Say it some other way.

Step off on the right foot— for this will determine the outcome

9

Have you ever jumped into a discussion with both feet, only to end up with both of them planted firmly in your mouth? Don't worry—for most people this is a familiar experience, but one that can be avoided.

It happens when we give too little thought to the 'whats', 'hows' and 'whys' of a conversation before we begin it. As a result, we fail to achieve the outcome we want. We spend our time poorly and fray our own and other people's tempers unnecessarily.

GET OFF ON THE RIGHT FOOT...

Communication Basic Number 4 in Chapter 1 was: *The way we begin our message often determines the outcome of the communication.* Yet (and you can be honest here): *how often do you really plan your first sentence or two before you begin a conversation?*

OH NO...

If you're like most busy people, the answer is probably: 'Not as often as I know I should'. And yet, spending a few moments thinking about your opening lines can save you time and frustration.

First think through your purpose: why are you communicating? What do you want to achieve? How do you want the discussion to proceed?

65

Once you are clear on this, you will be able to state, in your first sentence or two, the overall purpose of the conversation, and/or how you intend it to proceed. This is called **framing** a conversation: thinking before you speak so that you step off on the right foot.

Framing helps you in three important ways. First, it helps you to guide a conversation towards your desired result without being side-tracked. This saves time and tension.

Second, it helps you to align the other person's expectations of the conversation with your own. Third, it helps you present information in a way that avoids making the other person defensive, bristling at your first few words, or ignoring parts of your message.

Frame your conversations

As a frame encloses a picture, a framing statement encloses the conversation to come: what will be addressed and what won't be; what will be focused on and what won't be. As a frame draws attention to the contents of a picture, a framing statement draws attention to the main aspects of the conversation and sets limits to what will, and won't, be discussed.

When developing a framing statement, follow the KISS principle: Keep it Short and Simple.

Some types of framing statements

- **Boundaries**
  Establish what will and won't be focused on:

  'Today, we won't be talking about your overall job performance, which is excellent, but only about progress on the Customer Service Project.'

- **History**
  Review the key events that have a bearing on this conversation:

  'Sal, I'd like to talk about X, which, as you'll recall, we've discussed on three occasions this month. Last time we agreed . . .'

- **Purposes**
  Present your expectations of the meeting and check if the other person's expectations are similar or different:

  'Chris, I'd like to firm up some conclusions and a tentative plan on how best to proceed with this from here. How does that sound to you?'

- **Process**
  Present an overview of the types of information you would like to present and discuss:

  'Kim, I'd like to review our monthly budget and in particular, the expenditure areas of salaries and wages, rentals, consulting fees, and advertising.'

  or

  Outline how you would like the discussion to proceed:

  'I suggest that we begin with X; then move onto Y and then discuss C. How does that sound to you?'

- **Problem**
  State the categories of the problem and summarise the data, or facts, in the categories as you understand them:

  'Lee, I'd like to talk about timekeeping. My records show that you've been late to work three times and back late from lunch four times this past month. I have been keeping track of this because timekeeping is important to me. I'd like to discuss with you now any problems or difficulties that could be causing this and decide what we can do about it.'

  Use these singly or in combination to frame the discussion to come.

Practice makes perfect

Developing framing statements is a skill. The following incidents will help you practise. Read each, then jot down a short framing statement that you would feel comfortable with to open up a discussion. You'll find some model answers in Appendix 1; these are just examples and your answers will probably be as good— provided they're short and you can imagine yourself saying them.

1. Peter, one of your team members, has a habit of whispering to anyone sitting beside him for most of your team meetings. It really bugs you, because you need everyone's attention and input, and you think it annoys people trying to hear the others' contributions over Peter's whisperings. You open a discussion (in private) with Peter by saying:

   _____

   _____

   _____

2. Carla is a very talented co-worker. Unfortunately, some of your work hinges on Carla completing her work and passing it on to you. She is often late with it, and this makes you either rush and risk making mistakes, or miss your deadlines to your manager. You approach Carla and say:

   _____

   _____

   _____

3. Senior management has recently begun talking about achieving more work in less time. Manny is the manager of another department on your floor. His work team and yours work on different aspects of the same process and you have arranged a meeting

with Manny to discuss how your two teams could work together more smoothly to reduce some of the backlog and move work more quickly. You begin the meeting by saying:

_____

_____

_____

4. Sean is your manager. You've put forward a moderate capital expenditure proposal for your department for him to approve and you've had several meetings with him to go through the details; you know he's quite a slow decision-maker and you would like to speed up his decision if you can. You've asked for a meeting about it which you intend to open by saying:

_____

_____

_____

5. You supervise the management accounting section. Lately, your customers, that is, managers of other sections, have been suggesting that they would like the figures to come out more quickly. You've called a team meeting to explore how this might be done. You open the meeting by saying:

_____

_____

_____

6. Ellen is your assistant and, on the whole, is very able; however, you are concerned that she sometimes fails to meet routine deadlines. When you have discussed this on two occasions (three months ago at her performance appraisal, and again last month), she indicated that she is aware of this and felt that an

effort to be more organised would help. She has not shown any improvement and has missed several routine deadlines over the last few weeks. You begin this meeting by saying:

_____

_____

_____

When you open a discussion with a framing statement, you may stop there for a reply or you may decide to continue. Your judgment and observations of the other person's body language will tell you what to do.

Remember the WIFM factor

As early as you can in a conversation, even in the framing statement, work in a WIFM: What's In It For Me? (The 'Me' refers to the other person: why should the other person listen? What are the benefits to the other person?) If you can give a _reason_ to listen, people will do so more readily and, usually, more open-mindedly and enthusiastically.

This might mean stating the benefits you are proposing to them. Or it might mean appealing to something that interests them or engaging their desire to co-operate. Your knowledge of the person and the situation will help you to provide an appealing WIFM.

More practice!

Look again at the six practice situations above. On the next page, jot down possible WIFMs you could bring out early in the discussion. (You might get some ideas from Appendix 1.)

1. _____

2. _____

3. _____

4. _____

5. _____

6. _____

Be subtle when introducing a WIFM!

Appendix 1
Model framing answers
for practice exercises

1. 'Peter, I'd like to have a word with you about our team meetings. I've noticed that you often talk quietly to the person next to you and this bothers me because I really want everyone's input to be heard by the whole team.'

   You've decided not to mention Peter's whispering as annoyance to others because this is only a guess on your part. You've told Peter what you *do* want, not what you *don't* want.

2. 'Carla, have you got a minute? I'd like to have a chat about something that bothers me a lot.'

   At this point, you might deliver an 'I' statement (see Chapter 11.) You can't *force* Carla to change her work habits but you *can* point out how they affect you.

3. 'Thanks for getting together with me, Manny. We both know that management is keen to reduce the time it takes to get things done and at the same time, increase throughput. I think that between us, we'll be able to come up with a plan to do that. If you're agreeable, I'd like to talk about ways our two teams could work together to reduce lead time through our departments. I thought we might bounce a few ideas around ourselves and then perhaps call a meeting

73

of our work teams to see what ideas they have. How does that sound to you?'

The key here is working together to make improvements.

4. 'Thanks for seeing me about my expenditure proposal, Sean. I'd like to spend a few minutes on why I've put it to you and summarise its details. Then I thought we could work out the pros and cons of the proposal and list any concerns you might still have. What I'd hoped for is to make sure you have all the information you need to make a decision on it.'

   (*We're trying to put gentle pressure on Sean without making him feel defensive, uncomfortable or rushed.*)

5. 'Thank you for coming. I've asked you here to get some ideas on how we can speed up getting the figures out to each of our customer departments more quickly. I've spoken with each of the department managers, who agree that a reduction in turn-around from three weeks to two would be very helpful to them. First, I'd like to make a list on the board of the things that slow us down. Who can suggest anything?'

   (*Notice the tone is not 'You'll have to do it faster or better'; it's 'How can we improve?' This is more likely to lead to co-operation and ideas.*)

6. 'Ellen, it's missed-deadline discussion time again, I'm sorry to say. When we discussed this at your performance appraisal and again last month, you indicated that you felt you needed to be more organised. I'd like to hear what changes you've made to your working habits to become more organised and see if there's anything I can do to help. We've really got to come to grips with this.'

   We're treating this as a problem to be solved together; what, if anything, has she done to improve her organisation? What help might she need from you? If she has improved her organisation, is there some other explanation for missed deadlines?

WIFMs

Here are some WIFMs you could bring out in early in the discussion:

1. More respect or acceptance from other team members; not getting 'hassled' by you.

2. Smoother flow of work through the department; personal pride in meeting deadlines; helping you out (it might not have occurred to Carla that she was causing you a problem). At the very least, you'll feel better for having aired your concern.

3. You'll both gain some kudos with senior management for improved results; team participation is good for morale.

4. Approval will mean better results from your department which, in turn, will make Sean look good. He will feel quite comfortable with his decision because he will have all the facts he needs.

5. By cutting out wasted effort, repeated work, bottle-necks, and so on, their jobs will become much easier and more hassle-free; they'll have an opportunity to participate in improving the overall process that includes their jobs.

6. A chance for Ellen to improve the one poor area of her performance and become excellent in all aspects of her job; an opportunity to improve a critical job skill (self-organisation).

Choose your words for clarity and power

Words

The content of any message, as we've seen, is made up of far more than the words we use. This is not to say that words are not important—they are.

We can choose words that are aggressive or compliant, neutral or emotive, clear or vague, courteous or challenging, depending on our purpose. *We have a choice.*

Because of their effect on the message received, choose your words with care; don't use them thoughtlessly or through mere habit.

77

The power of words

Suppose you want to explain to someone that you're concerned that their rapid, abrupt manner on the telephone might leave customers with a poor impression of the organisation. You could say something like:

> 'Jan, you're too abrupt on the telephone; you'll need to be more professional—starting now!'

This approach is likely to upset Jan instead of encouraging her to soften her telephone manner. The lack of clarity is unhelpful, too: would Jan think she was being 'abrupt'? What do 'abrupt' and 'more professional' mean? It's unlikely that Jan set out to be either 'unprofessional' or 'abrupt' and therefore, to ask her to be less of either is pointless. The 'starting now!' sounds too strong and is unlikely to achieve the results you want. 'Commanding', remember, is one of the 11 deadly sins of communication.

Let's introduce the conversation with a **frame**, such as:

> 'Jan, I am concerned about the way you speak to customers over the telephone and I'd like to discuss it with you; do you have some time now?'

We could make our message more specific by saying, for example:

> *'I've noticed that you speak quite quickly and I'm worried that this might make it difficult for some of the customers to follow you; after all, you know more about what you're talking about than they do.'*

'Also, you're very efficient and tend to give 'the bottom line' only; I think it might be more helpful to customers, Jan, if you were to round-out your discussions with a bit more background.'

This uses 'I' language (see Chapter 11) and offers suggestions for improvement (see Chapter 13). It is more likely to encourage Jan to be co-operative.

The only person who can choose to alter her telephone manner with customers is Jan. Commanding won't do it; all you can do is coach her and perhaps point out the results of altering versus not altering her telephone manner.

Words can create defensiveness and lead to arguments or they can be a positive influence

Much of our time as managers is devoted to influencing others and to modifying the actions or behaviours of others. Some of this is based on negative assessments that must be communicated.

There is a natural tendency, when trying to influence another person, to send signals, one of the three types of deadly communication sins. It's easy to become domineering, to command or threaten, to give unsolicited (and therefore unheard or ignored) advice.

The position we take can easily become one of superiority, which leads to patronising—another type of deadly sin. The sins of evaluating and labelling quickly follow.

This happens even if we attempt (on the surface) to be pleasant and helpful. Underneath we will be evaluative, superior, and certain. The more difficult or prolonged the interaction is and the less rapport we feel with the other person, the more pronounced these subconscious motives will become. Communication will begin to break down.

Energy will be focused on 'winning'; rather than listen, we will mentally prepare a rebuttal while the other person speaks. Frustration will mount. The communicators will become critical of each other; positions such as: 'I am right and you are clearly wrong, unreasonable, stubborn or downright stupid' will be taken.

The consequence of such a discussion is defensiveness, anger, hostility, eroded mutual respect, and a weak compromise or capitulation by one of the parties; the loser will have lost the battle but not the war.

How can we avoid this?

Carefully frame your messages and transmit them factually or descriptively, in neutral language, and in a neutral, non-judgmental tone of voice.

LISTEN with empathy and understanding, to see things from the other person's point of view.

This needs a genuine *desire* to gather as well as give good information, plus some skills: active listening skills, the ability to give good information, and skills in problem- solving. In this chapter we examine the words we choose to use to give good information.

Use neutral words

Think about the connotations these pairs of words have for you:

fashionable	receiving a lot of attention
flash in the pan	very popular
abrupt	quick, rapid
undependable	variable
woolly thinking	unclear

Those on the left have negative connotations while those on the right are *neutral, factual* or more *descriptive*. The same can be true for the phrases that we choose. Consider these:

You're lazy and irresponsible.	You've been late three times this week and although there's a lot of work in your in-basket, you're reading the newspaper.
You're wrong.	I disagree.
These figures are rubbish!	I need to be more certain about the way figures were arrived at.
Stop interrupting me!	Pat, I'm speaking *or* Please let me finish.

We can choose phrases that are emotive or imply a negative judgment or we can choose phrases that are neutral.

Similarly, we can choose a hostile tone of voice or one that is neutral and courteous.

The response to a loaded, emotion-laden word or a word or phrase with negative connotations and a hostile tone of voice is quite different from the response to a neutral, factual or descriptive word or phrase and tone of voice. The former is likely to provoke defensiveness, resentment and even

Stop and think before you speak—especially if you feel annoyed or angry. How can you get your message across in a way that discourages defensiveness and arguments?
Use *neutral language* and a *neutral tone of voice.*

hostility; a battle could result. The latter generally results in listening, fact-gathering and problem-solving.

Choose specific words

When we use a word, *we* know what it means. But do *others*?

> Both Humpty Dumpty and the Queen of Hearts declared: 'A word means just what I want it to mean—nothing more, nothing less' (or *words* to that effect). And that's about the size of it.

Unfortunately, what we mean, and what another person understands, can be quite different.

Take the word 'order', for instance. Spend a few seconds and jot down what this word means to you.

Order:

_____

_____

_____

You could have written down 1 of any of 15 definitions or more than 24 shades of meaning for that one word (some of which are listed in Appendix 2). We so often think we 'know', don't we?

See how many definitions to the word 'strike' you can think of:

Strike:

_____   _____   _____

_____   _____   _____

_____   _____   _____

_____   _____   _____

_____   _____   _____

(There are 13 definitions and over 18 connotations; some of these are listed in Appendix 2.)

Words can make communication an uncertain business.

*Choose words that meet the requirements of the **Six Cs**:*

> *CLEAR*
>
> *CONCISE*
>
> *COMPLETE*
>
> *COURTEOUS*
>
> *CORRECT*
>
> *CONCRETE* (specific)

Words must be **clear**. You must be clear in your own mind about what you want or what you intend to convey. Choose words that convey the message clearly to the other person.

Apply the KISS principle: Keep It Short and Simple. Be **concise** so that people don't lose interest and let their attention wander. People can remember only seven (plus or minus two) pieces of information at a time, so don't add to the mental burden with extra words.

At the same time, be as **complete** as your message requires. Ask questions to check understanding. Watch the other person's body language for clues about whether you are giving too much, or not enough, information.

Be **courteous** because 'behaviour breeds behaviour'. Be **correct** and be **concrete** to avoid confusion.

If you have any reason to believe that your meaning or intention will be misunderstood, make it clear precisely what you mean, intend, or expect. Don't leave it to chance or to guesswork'.

Ask for feedback too, to hear for yourself that the message received is the same as the message intended.

Speak your words clearly and slowly enough to be understood

Having chosen words that are clear, concise, complete, courteous, correct, and concrete, speak clearly and slowly enough to be understood.

Make your words precise, memorable and powerful

All of this will help the meaning received match the meaning you intend. The next task is to choose your words to persuade, to have 'punch' and power. There are six specific things you can do.

Make word pictures

One picture is worth 1000 words. Most people in societies such as ours tend to think in pictures. Use this knowledge. Make your words paint pictures. Help people form the mental pictures that *you* want them to. This can be used for feelings, sensations, and sounds, too. Use words to create the images, feelings, and sounds you want. Don't leave it to chance if you don't have to.

'I want our customers to feel like guests in our home' is more precise and memorable than 'Treat the customers nicely'.

Support your words with visual aids

Show *and* tell. If we *hear* something, chances are that we'll remember 10 to 15 per cent of it a day or so later. If we *see* it, we'll recall 30 to 35 per cent of it. Add the two together and we have a fairly memorable communication.

Here's another interesting statistic: 83 to 87 per cent of everything that goes into our brains goes in visually; only 11 per cent goes in aurally. Once again, the eyes have it. Increase the power of your words by showing the eyes, too. In fact, bring into play as many senses as you can for precise and memorable communication.

Give demonstrations

Show *and* tell, again. This time so that people can see exactly what happens, precisely how something works, or what exactly is to be done. This is a much more memorable form of communication.

Provide story-type examples

Story-type examples and specific examples are easy to remember. People can relate to and recall these better than straightforward instructions or information.

Talk in language the other person uses and can relate to

formal	informal
technical terms	everyday terms
long words	short words

People have characteristic ways of speaking. If you can include similar types of words, you will make it easier for others to understand and relate to what you're saying and make it easier for them to receive your message in the way you intend.

Phrase things the way the other person does

Watch and listen to how the other person uses words and phrases sentences. The field of neurolinguistic programming (NLP) teaches us to watch and listen for four basic modes, or representational systems, of communication:

1. **Visual** (seeing)

The words visual people use convey lots of visual images; pictures are important: **'How does that look to you?'**

They:

- look up a lot when they think
- speak quickly and in higher tones
- gesture with hands held high
- breathe rapidly, shallowly, or irregularly, high in the chest.

2. **Auditory** (hearing)

The words of auditory people convey lots of sound; sound is important: **'How does that sound to you?'**

They:

- look to the side a lot when they think
- speak with resonance, slowly, and in lower tones
- gesture with hands at mid-torso
- breathe slower, evenly, in the middle of the chest.

3. Kinaesthetic (feeling, touch)

The words of kinaesthetic people convey lots of feelings and touch sensations; touch is important: **'How does that feel to you?'**

They:

- look down and to their right a lot when they think
- speak in deep tones
- gesture a lot, holding their hands lower, and they touch themselves a lot
- breathe from the abdomen.

4. Digital (logical/analytical)

The words of digital people convey the idea of thought and reflection; the words themselves are important: **'Does that make sense to you?'**

They:

- look down and to their left a lot when thinking
- speak in well-modulated, slow-paced, low tones
- gesture minimally.

This does not describe four 'types' of people, but describes the four most common ways that people use to convey and sift information. Most of us use all these representational systems in varying combinations.

However, we usually have a favourite representational system that we excel at and trust more than the others. We need to be able to operate in all of them, though, if we are to have the flexibility to 'connect' with people when we communicate with them.

Visual words

Listen for these visual words used on their own or in phrases and watch the eyes of the visual person.

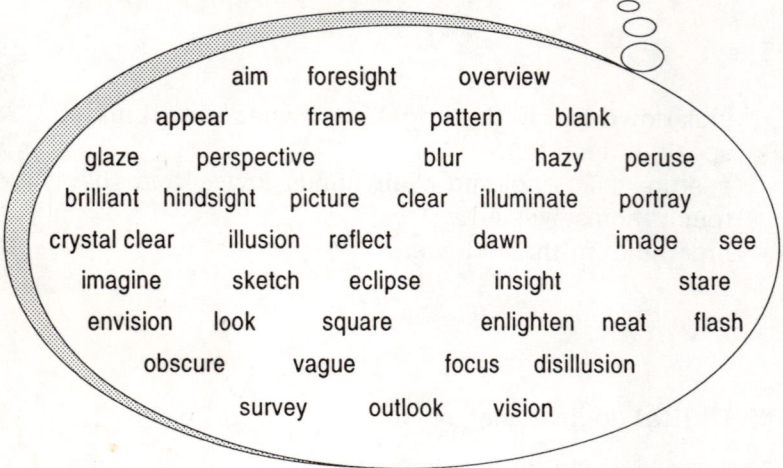

aim foresight overview
appear frame pattern blank
glaze perspective blur hazy peruse
brilliant hindsight picture clear illuminate portray
crystal clear illusion reflect dawn image see
imagine sketch eclipse insight stare
envision look square enlighten neat flash
obscure vague focus disillusion
survey outlook vision

Auditory words

Listen for these auditory words used on their own or in phrases and watch the eyes of the auditory person.

acclaim cry hear
aloud debate mention announce
decry muffle articulate describe
attune dialogue overtone babble discordant
propose beat discuss question be heard
dissonance rebuff music blank out echo resounding
boom exclaim retort call frequency snap
chord groan speechless click grumble
talk contact harmony
tune

Kinaesthetic words

Listen for these kinaesthetic words used on their own or in phrases and watch the eyes of the kinaesthetic person.

activate   complacent   fumble
get hold of   active   connect   grasp
agitate   delightful   hand   anxious   disenchanted
handle   backing   drive   happy   balance   embarrassed
hungry   blend   emotional   impact   bliss   energetic
irritate   block   equilibrium   link   bond   exasperated
loose   bounce   fall   manipulate   calm   fed up
massage   carry   finger   rub   cemented   sticky
frustrated   touch   crawl

Digital words

Digital words evoke thoughts more than pictures, sounds or feelings. Although specific, logical and accurate, they can be quite 'dry'. Watch the eyes of the digital person.

act   conceive   know   ambiguous
consider   learn   appreciate   decide   motivate
associate   discern   perceive   aware   distinct   ponder
be conscious   emphasise   precede   believe
experience   pretend   blend   generate   process
calibrate   guess   read   cancel   insensitive   recall
choice   integrate   recognise   comprehend
intent   understand

Use people's names

Finally, a name might be a word, but, to paraphrase Dale Carnegie, the sweetest word to anyone's ears is the sound of their own name. Dale Carnegie was right. Using peoples' names gets their attention. It makes them feel more positive towards you and your message. But don't overdo it. Use a person's name too often and it's just an empty, slick technique.

Appendix 2
Some word meanings:
'order' and 'strike'

'Order'

align
arrange
array
assemble
category
command
contract
demand
dictate

edict
genus
grouping
instruction
line
mandate
method
normal
pattern

rank
religious fraternity
requisition
reserve
row
sequence
suitable
to book

'Strike'

ambush
assault
attack
blow
boycott
coin
cuff

delete
dispute
hit
impose
knock
mint

picket
punch
raid
smite
stamp
walk-out

Speak for yourself, not the world— 'I' language and assertiveness

11

An important skill in giving good information—saying how things are from your point of view—is the skill of assertiveness. Using 'I' language is an important aspect of assertiveness. It is about 'owning your messages' or 'speaking for yourself, not the world'. Using 'I' helps you to communicate in a very clear and direct way. People don't need to be on guard when communicating with you. They don't need to guess what you *really* mean.

Own your messages

You've heard the phrase 'Everyone knows'? This is an example of *not* owning a message. People can hide what they think or believe behind what other people think or believe. 'I think . . .' and 'I believe . . .' are examples of owning your message.

Speak for yourself

To use 'We think . . .' or 'We'd like . . .', unless you have been elected the official spokesperson for a group, is an example of speaking for everyone. It is hiding

what you want to say behind what you are suggesting
other people think or want. 'I think . . .' or 'It seems to
me . . .' is speaking for yourself.

Ask real questions, not pseudo questions

People also hide behind what are called 'pseudo questions'.
Communications are rife with these, so much so that
we can put pseudo questions into six categories.

Coercive questions

These are leading questions that narrow or limit the
possible answers and lure the other person into giving
the answer you want.

'Don't you think . . . ?'

'. . . , Right?'

'Wouldn't you rather . . . [do this] . . .?'

What we really mean is 'I think', or 'Let's . . . [do this] . . .'

'Gotcha' questions

These are the questions that indirectly (and seemingly innocently) point out a weakness in the other person or show up mistakes they have made.

'Didn't you say . . . [and look how wrong you were!]'.

'What time did you get in?' (in front of the boss, knowing the person was late).

'If I remember, you were in favour of . . . [that failed initiative]'.

Hypothetical questions

These are an indirect, backdoor way of making a statement.

'If you were in charge here, wouldn't you . . ?'

What we really mean is: *'If I were in charge here, I'd do it this way . . .'*

Imperative questions

These turn a demand or command into an apparent request.

'Have you done anything about . . .?'

'When will you be finished with . . .?'

'When are you going to . . .?'

What we really mean is *'I think you should have seen to . . . by now'*, or *'I need you to have finished . . .'*, or *'I think you should have finished . . .'*, or *'I think you should do it soon'*.

Screened questions

Rather than starting with what *we* think or want, we ask the other person what *they* think or want (with our fingers crossed hoping that what they want will be the same as what we want).

'Where do you want to go?'

'What do you think our first move should be?'

'What do you want to do?'

What we really mean is *'I'd like to go here'*, or *'I think X should be our first move'* or *'Let's do this'*.

Set-up questions

These are double-whammy coercive questions, usually asked of people junior in rank. We set them up, then put them down. (Skilled managers can do it with their peers, too, and succeed for a while.)

'Wouldn't you agree . . . [timekeeping is important]' . . . ? 'Then why are you late?'

'Pseudo questions' make people feel uncomfortable and put them on guard because they intuitively know that there is more behind such questions than meets the eye.

If you do not own your messages, but speak for the world, or ask pseudo questions, the result will be guessing games, defensiveness, inaccurate assumptions, and crossed communication wires.

Speaking for yourself, owning your messages and asking questions for information, clarification and to check understanding, lead to clear communication. They are skills and must be built on a foundation of empathy, rapport, and respect for other people.

These skills encourage a two-way sharing of ideas, opinions, and beliefs; they help information to flow freely and guard against contradictory messages. Such skills lead to giving and gathering good information and are part of a range of skills which generally come under the heading of 'assertiveness'.

HAVE YOU SEEN MY WATCH?

Give good information—be assertive

People are born with instincts. We breathe; we close our eyes and duck or protect our heads if something flies through the air towards us; we stand our ground and fight, or turn tail and run if we feel threatened.

Learning assertion skills can override some instincts. We can learn to catch a ball without shutting our eyes or ducking or protecting our heads.

It would probably be impossible to learn to hold our breath until we dropped dead since our instinct for self-preservation is so strong. However, we can learn to breathe through snorkels or oxygen masks; we can learn to modify even our strongest instincts.

Similarly, we can learn assertiveness skills and use them to override, or at least modify, our instinctive fight–flight behaviour.

That instinctive behaviour was useful for our early ancestors, and is now of very limited use as the life-threatening situations the instinct was designed for are few and far between.

The **fight instinct** leads to aggressive communication: the win–lose behaviour of force. It leads to hostility, anger, and resentment.

The **flight instinct** leads to passive, submissive communication: the lose–lose avoid or lose–win accommodate behaviour. This also leads to bad feelings and damages relationships.

Assertiveness is a skill which must be learned. It is not inborn as aggression and submission are. Mastering assertiveness is essential for effective communication.

Assertion skills

When people first begin to practise assertive communication they often overstep the boundary into aggression. It is as if they are so carried away with their new-found ability to state their own point of view that they forget other people also have a right to state their points of view. The empathy and mutual respect aspect of assertion is often overlooked.

The best way to learn assertion skills is to begin practising them in safe surroundings and with people who will feel able to tell you if you have overstepped the boundary into aggression.

If you would like to develop your assertion skills, read the descriptions of the skills on the following page. Watch people as they communicate. Choose one, two or three people who you believe communicate assertively. Emulate them.

You will recognise assertive people from the 'I' language they use ('I think', 'I feel', 'I want', 'I need', 'I'd like') and their brief, clear, and direct statements; their suggestions which are not weighted with 'advice', 'commands', 'shoulds' or 'oughts'; their concern for

---

Assertive skills and body language

Verbally assertive people:
- make statements that are honest, clear, brief and to the point;
- use 'I' statements: 'I'd like . . .', 'I appreciate . . .', 'I think . . .';
- distinguish between fact and opinion;
- ask don't tell;
- offer improvement suggestions, not advice or commands;
- offer constructive criticism, free of blame, assumptions, or 'shoulds';
- ask questions to find out the thoughts and feelings of others;
- respect the rights of others as well as their own rights;
- communicate mutual respect where the needs of two people conflict, and look for mutually acceptable solutions.

Non-verbally assertive people:
- make appropriate eye contact;
- sit or stand firmly and comfortably erect;
- gesture openly and to support their comments;
- speak in a clear, steady, firm tone of voice;
- maintain open, steady, relaxed facial expressions, smiling when pleased, frowning when angry;
- speak at a steady, even pace, emphasising key words, with few awkward hesitations;

Assertive people are often described as:

Honest	Concerned for others	Relaxed
Flexible	Open	Tolerant
Joyous	Confident	Accountable
Trusting	Leaders	Mature

---

other people; their constructive criticisms, free of blame or assumptions; their relaxed, flexible and open behaviour; their confidence and acceptance of others and of points of view different from their own. Such ways of communicating are the hallmarks of assertive people.

Use these assertive people as role models. Watch what they say and how they say it. Look at their body language. Do what they do.

It is important to remember that you need to use the techniques outlined below in a way that respects the other person and shows willingness to hear their point of view. Giving only your own point of view is aggressive, not assertive.

When you find yourself in a situation calling for assertive communication, ask yourself how your role models would handle it. Then do it. 'Fake it till you make it' it a good motto for practising assertive communication skills.

Don't be side-tracked

If someone is ignoring your main message or trying to sidetrack you, you may find it necessary to use the **broken-record technique**. Like a broken record, you calmly repeat your main message, as often as necessary until it is heard.

You may also want to state your understanding of the other person's point as a way of showing that you have heard it. Then repeat your main message.

This doesn't mean brushing aside what the other person has to say; equally, don't let them brush aside what you have to say.

Lee: *'Sam, I'd like to discuss your timekeeping. As you know, because we've discussed it twice before, I can't afford to have you coming in late in the mornings.'*

Sam: *'Oh, I'm sorry about this morning. I had trouble with the car. It's been giving me a lot of bother lately, and. . .'*

Lee: *'I understand that. I still need you here on time in the mornings.'*

Sam: *'Well, I always work through lunch hours.'*

Lee:	*'Yes and I appreciate that. I need you here on time in the mornings, too.'*
Sam:	*'Well Jan was late yesterday and you didn't say anything to her!'*
Lee:	*'Jan had spoken to me before. Sam, what are you going to do about getting here on time in the morning from now on?'*

The aim of this technique is to make your point without making an enemy.

The broken-record technique is also a good way to say 'no' without making an enemy.

Tony:	*'Jan, can you give me a hand compiling this report?'*
Jan:	*'I can't; I'm really snowed under myself and I'm rushing to meet a 4 o'clock deadline.'*
Tony:	*'But this won't take long.'*
Jan:	*'I understand that, and I really can't spare the time.'*
Tony:	*'Oh, please, Jan, I'd really appreciate it.'*
Jan:	*'I really can't help you out just now.'*

You can't blame someone for asking. And *you* have a right to say 'no'.

Look for a compromise

In Chapter 6 we looked at how to achieve win–win solutions. Sometimes, rather than saying 'no', collaborating or working towards a win–win compromise is a better option. Sometimes you can combine this with the technique of broken record.

Tony:	*'Jan, can you give me a hand compiling this report?'*

Jan: *'I can't; I'm really snowed under myself and I'm rushing to meet a 4 o'clock deadline.'*

Tony: *'But this won't take long.'*

Jan: *'I understand that and I really can't spare the time right now. I'll have some time to help you with it tomorrow if you like.'*

Tony: *'Oh, come on, Jan! I've promised I'd have it ready first thing tomorrow morning.'*

Jan: *'I'd be happy to help you after I've got my work done for my own 4 o'clock deadline. How's that?'*

Tony: *'Thanks Jan, I really appreciate it.'*

Deal with criticism assertively

Sometimes people attack you or criticise you. Criticism is often valuable because it can provide you with important information worthy of your consideration.

If you need to find out more about the criticism, perhaps to decide if it's worth listening to. The technique of **negative inquiry** is very helpful for drawing out more specific information.

Keep probing the person's criticisms until they are clear to you. For example:

Chris: *'Pat, I'd like to see a more thorough job on that Jells report.'*

Pat: *'I'm not sure what you mean by "more thorough" ', Chris.'*

Chris: *'Well, basically, I'd like to see a lot more detail about how you reached your conclusions.'*

Pat:	'Okay, I can easily add that information. Is there anything else I could do to make it better?'
Chris:	'Maybe a bit more supporting evidence would be good.'
Pat:	'Fine, I can add a couple of tables as an appendix. Would that do it?'
Chris:	'Yes, I think that about covers it. I'd really like to have it by Friday; would that be possible?'

Chapter 19 gives additional information on *questioning for clarity*.

Don't get involved in discussions if you don't want to

Sometimes we don't want to get involved in a discussion, at least at that moment. Or we might disagree with the criticism but want to avoid an argument: 'Yes you are', 'No I'm not', 'Yes you are . . .'

This is when the technique of **fogging** can be used. When you 'fog' a criticism, you acknowledge that *perhaps* it is true (and perhaps it isn't). For example:

Fred:	'Paul, that presentation you gave to the executive committee was chronic!'
Paul:	'Maybe I could have made a better job of it.'
Fred:	'I'll say! Boy was it off.'
Paul:	'I see your point!'
Fred:	'Yeah, it sure was boring.'
Paul:	'I can see you might have found it boring. Maybe next time I'll spruce it up a bit.'
Fred:	'I hope you do!'

It sometimes helps to repeat the gist of the criticism first.

At other times, we may know that there are grounds for the criticism yet we do not wish to discuss it at that time. This is when the technique of **negative assertion** can be useful.

To prevent becoming involved in a long discussion, acknowledge the criticism without adding to it or detracting from it.

Fred: *'Paul, that address you gave to the executive committee was chronic!'*

Paul: *'Yeah, I know.'*

Fred: *'Boy was it off!'*

Paul: *'I've certainly given better talks!'*

Fred: *'It was so boring!'*

Paul: *'Yes, and I know what I'll do next time to make it more interesting.'*

Fred: *'Glad to hear it!'*

Talk about yourself assertively

Assertive skills don't merely fend off unreasonable requests or deal with criticism. They also help us to talk about ourselves, our thoughts, and our feelings.

We've already explored **owning messages**; to this we can add **owning feelings**. Here are some examples:

'I feel that we're going around in circles. Perhaps we need to try a different approach.'

'I could really do with a break now. How about you?'

'I'm not following what you're saying.'

'I'm confused.'

'I feel pretty angry about this and I'd like to discuss it with you later.'

'I feel I'm being pushed into a corner here. I need some time to think about what you're asking.'

'I feel uncomfortable discussing this right now. Would you mind if we discuss it later?'

Sharing what is happening to us personally is often very helpful for getting a discussion 'unstuck', strengthening relationships, and accomplishing tasks.

Assertive communication is more than a set of techniques. It is a set of skills based on mutual respect. It involves the giving and the gathering of good information: the ability to say how it is on your side and the willingness to hear how it is on the other's side.

Speaking for yourself; owning your messages; dealing with criticism; saying 'no' when you want to; showing respect for the other person: all these can dramatically improve any communication.

Don't masquerade your opinion as facts

A wise man once pointed out the distinction between **fact**, **fantasy** and **folklore**. 'Facts', he said, 'are facts. Although we like to pretend otherwise, there are not as many facts around as we might think'.

Opinions are what he referred to as 'fantasy'. 'We have a bad habit', he said, 'of masquerading our opinions as facts. And they're not; they're only opinions, our little fantasies'.

'Folklore is what we know as hearsay: the grapevine, the rumour mill. And as we all know', he said 'most of this is folklore'.

So, here is his advice:

1. *Be sure of your facts and never present anything as a fact that isn't a fact.*

2. *When you're stating an opinion, let people know that it's your opinion. Own it. Don't masquerade it as a fact.*

3. *Don't deal in folklore.*

4. *When someone is telling you something, listen carefully and ask questions to distinguish between fact, fantasy, and folklore.*

This is not to say that opinions are not valuable. They are. If we didn't hold opinions, we could never make decisions. As managers, it's important that we draw on other people's opinions. They are important sources of information and should be considered. Just don't masquerade them as facts or confuse them with facts!

It is the responsibility of the sender of information to distinguish between fact, fantasy, and folklore. This is nice in theory; sadly, it is seldom done in practice.

So, we need to be vigilant. As receivers, it is important that we listen carefully and ask questions so that we can distinguish between fact, fantasy, and folklore. The difference could be important.

Be explicit about assumptions

While we're distinguishing between orders of information, let's not overlook the ubiquitous assumption.

It's easy to get caught up in assumptions and treat them as facts. Many an expensive and embarrassing decision has been based on incorrect assumptions that no-one bothered to check.

To check assumptions, you need to explicitly state them. This is seldom easy; most assumptions are reached almost instantaneously and often unconsciously as the brain tries to make sense of confusing and often contradictory information.

Always ask yourself: What assumptions am I making here? Is there any way to check them? Are other people involved likely to be working from the same assumptions, or might they have made different assumptions? Would a different set of assumptions be equally valid?

Ask, don't tell

13

We've seen how telling, demanding, commanding, forcing and so on draw resistant responses. The spirit of 'ask, don't tell' overcomes this.

'Ask, don't tell' is based on mutual respect. The door is open for discussion and there is the possibility of collaborating or reaching a compromise. The other person has choices.

You don't want to allow options or choice? You really have no choice! Options and choices always exist. Able-minded adults are always free to do as you ask, or not; or to do as you tell them to, or not. The most you can do is point out the consequences to them of not doing as you ask or tell.

It might even be necessary to get heavy and use the Change—Time—Consequence formula:

Change	*'if not **this** change,*
Time	*by **this** time,*
Consequence	*the consequence will be **this**'.*

It is up to the other person to decide whether or not to change their behaviour. At least they will make an informed decision.

Since telling invites resistance, why not *ask*? As communicators, we want to choose the option of least resistance.

Always ask; never demand.
Offer suggestions for improvement.
Turn complaints into requests.

This is an easy habit to form once you see how well it works.

Instead of: 'I want that ready by midday!' try: *'I really need to have that done by midday; will that be possible for you?'* (If the person says 'no', you may have to reach a compromise or adjust some of their work priorities.)

Instead of: 'Don't do that!' say: *'You'll find it easier [or safer)] to do it this way.'*

Instead of: 'I hate it when you do that!' try: *'Would you mind doing X instead?'* or *'I'd rather you did X instead.'*

No demands, no commands, no threats—less resistance.

Use 'I' statements for the big stuff

Another way of asking, not telling, is to offer an 'I' statement. This is another assertive communication technique. 'I' statements are a way of specifying a person's behaviour and stating how it affects you or why it is important. Because they are so powerful, a request to someone to alter their behaviour, communicated as an 'I' statement, has a better chance of success than a command, threat, complaint, hint, or other non-assertive form of request.

'I' statements help you to express your point of view calmly without blaming the other person or treading on their toes as would, for example, a demand that they 'mend their ways'. They help you communicate clearly and

When you feel annoyed with someone or want to ask them not to do something, make an 'I' statement.

cleanly and in a way that won't make the other person wary or defensive. 'I' statements increase the chances of achieving a result you want.

'I' statements

Step 1   What you see or hear or what you think the facts are (**no blame—neutral words**):

                     'When you . . .'

Step 2   How you feel (*not* what you think):

                     'I am (frustrated, annoyed, angry, thrilled, over-joyed, hurt)'

Step 3   Why it matters, the tangible or intangible effects of the first point:

                     'Because . . .'

Step 1, stating the facts or the behaviour *must* be done using specific, non-judgmental, neutral words. Make sure the behaviour you specify is observable and not an interpretation. Keep it brief.

> Juggle around the order of Steps 1, 2, and 3. Say what is most important first. *But use all three Steps!*

In Step 2, talk about its effect on you. *Not* what you think about it ('I think that's totally irresponsible of you'). State how you *feel* about it ('I feel really let down'). If you can substitute the words 'I think' for 'I feel', start again.

'I feel you are not pulling your weight' = *'I don't think you are pulling your weight'*. Yes, but how do you *feel* about it? Let down, angry, wishing she were not on your team?

Then use Step 3, talk about the consequences or tangible effects of the behaviour. Be clear, courteous, and factual. This is not a demand or a threat—'. . . and if you don't stop it, I'll . . .'—but some information—*'If this doesn't improve by such and such a date, I will have to give you a written warning'*, or *'I'm worried that our customers will get the wrong idea and we'll lose business as a result'*. This helps the person make an informed decision about whether or not to change their behaviour.

Here's an alternative 'I' statement that can be used with more straightforward issues.

An alternative 'I' statement

Step 1   What you see or hear or what you think the facts are:

              'When you . . .'

Step 2   How you feel (*not* what you think):

              'I am (frustrated, annoyed, angry, thrilled, overjoyed)'

Step 3   What you would prefer instead:

              'I'd prefer that . . .' or *'And what I'd like is . . .'*

In this example, instead of stating the consequences, you have stated what you want. This is acceptable for obvious issues but not for more complex issues.

Frame   *'Lee, I'd like to discuss this morning's meeting with you.*

Step 1   *You interjected several times before I had finished speaking and as a result, I lost my train of thought.*

Step 2   *I also felt quite intimidated and embarrassed.*

Step 3   *I'd really like to finish what I'm saying. How about it?'*

Take care with 'I' statements. Constructing them often takes practice at first. There is a fine line between an 'I' statement and an attempt to impose your values or wishes on another person. Use them as an opener, not a resolver.

Think through carefully what you want to say and jot it down. You might not say exactly what you wrote, but this process is very helpful. By writing it down you will clarify your 'I' statement to make sure it meets the criteria described above. You can also learn a lot about yourself from composing 'I' statements.

Use 'I' statements to strengthen behaviour you want, too

Don't get the impression that 'I' statements are just for 'tellings-off'. They're particularly effective forms of praise and encourage more of the same behaviour.

Step 1   *'Liz, that presentation was fantastic. You looked relaxed and comfortable up there and all the key points came across loud and clear. Your visual aids were particularly good because they were easy to read and emphasised your main points.*

Step 2   *I was really proud to have you on my team.*

Step 3   *Judging from their enthusiastic response I think the board will approve the proposal.'*

Step 1 spells out precisely what was good; it shows Liz what is important to you and this lets her know what to focus on in the future. Step 2 makes her feel great and boosts her confidence. And step 3 indicates that her effort is worthwhile.

With an 'I' statement, you say what you want to say. After delivering an 'I' statement, go straight into active listening (Chapter 17). This helps the other person to say what they want to say. Combine 'I' statements and active listening to help solve problems.

Use 'I' statements to encourage the behaviour you want.

Never say what you like (or don't) without saying why you like it (or don't)

Giving feedback to people, whether positive or negative, is an important management skill. Take a look at the different types of feedback available to you.

Three types of feedback

There are three types of feedback: positive, negative, and none at all.

Positive feedback can be general or specific. **General positive feedback**, like *'You're terrific to work with'* or *'I value your professionalism'* makes people feel good—about you and about themselves. If you are sincere and have credibility with the other person, it will increase their self-esteem, and strengthen the relationship between you.

> Use general positive feedback every once in a while to strengthen relationships and make everyone feel good.

Specific positive feedback, such as *'You're terrific to work with because you always do what you say you'll do'* or *'I really value the way you can calm an irate customer without getting upset yourself'* is good for making sure that the specific behaviour referred to is repeated.

117

Use specific positive feedback soon after a behaviour if you want it to be repeated. Do this regularly to build good performance among co-workers.

Negative feedback can also be general or specific. **General negative feedback**, like *'Boy, are you dumb!'* or *'Leave me alone!'* or *'You're not trying hard enough!'* makes people feel bad. It lowers self-esteem and erodes relationships.

Don't use general negative feedback, ever.

Specific negative feedback, such as *'You're not doing it the way I showed you'* or *'You were late again this morning'* merely tells people what not to do. Unless specific negative feedback is given carefully, it often fails to eliminate the undesired behaviour and it can easily result in 'playing-it-safe' behaviour.

We make mistakes and we learn from them. When it is necessary to provide negative feedback, make sure it is offered in a way that will help people to learn.

Use 'I' statements and the other suggestions from Chapter 13, and the general guidelines outlined below, whenever you offer specific negative feedback.

Remember to follow up specific negative feedback with specific positive feedback when an improvement occurs.

When there has been **No feedback** at all people wither up and die, psychologically. It sends the message that *'You're not important and neither is what you do'*. If people think what they do doesn't matter, they'll lose interest in it and stop trying to do it well. Performance can erode to the point where negative feedback becomes necessary.

Don't give *No feedback!* That is, don't ignore people—recognise them and what they do in a positive way.

Being heard

Think of feedback as a mirror, a means by which you can offer your observations about another person's behaviour. You can go one step further and reflect both the behaviour and its effects on you and/or your feelings or reactions to that behaviour.

Offer feedback in a way that the receiver can 'hear' it and accept it. Here are some guidelines to achieve this.

Be specific

Using an example from an earlier chapter, 'discourteous' or 'abrupt' might mean something to you but probably means something quite different to the person you accuse of being 'discourteous' or 'abrupt'. As these words are general and open to interpretation, they are not much use. 'Speaking rapidly', 'not making much eye contact', 'continuing to do other things while speaking to someone' are specific.

If you are specific when providing feedback, people know clearly what you approve or disapprove of. They will know specifically what to continue or to stop doing.

Address behaviour, not your interpretation or 'labels'

'Lazy' and 'bad attitude' are meaningless general terms, and are labels or negative interpretations. 'I never see you helping the others when you're finished with your work; what I do see is that you seem to go for smoko'; 'you are walking slowly and shuffling your feet along the floor'; 'you allow the phone to ring more than four times before answering it'. Information given like this is easier to hear because it addresses specific behaviours without interpreting or labelling them.

Use specific words and phrases that clearly describe a behaviour, in preference to those that are your interpretations, impressions, or 'mental shorthand'.

Be constructive

Some people give feedback as if they're trying to unload all their hassles at once; that might make them feel better, but it is unhelpful to the receiver. 'You do *this*, and *this*, and *that* and you also do *this*, and while we're at it . . .'. Such dumping creates defensive and resentful responses.

Others tear people down when they give them feedback, as if tearing down the receiver will build up the sender. To be helpful, the receiver must sense that the feedback is offered constructively, in a spirit of support and encouragement.

Aim to empower and motivate people when you give them feedback.

Formulate your feedback along the lines of 'I think you would be more effective if . . .' or 'You might consider trying . . .' whenever you can.

Let people feel free to accept or reject your feedback.

Be balanced—give positive as well as negative feedback. This shows you have objectivity and it helps people to see a truer picture of themselves.

Be realistic

The behaviour that your feedback concerns must be something the person can deal with. If someone is so shy that they have great difficulty dealing with customers, no feedback, no matter how constructive or helpful ('You'll really need to learn to relax and speak to customers better') will help.

This also means you must offer 'fresh' feedback, not 'old' feedback. Don't save up comments for months or for the annual performance appraisal. Dealing with troublesome matters immediately, after a moment's thought, is usually the best policy. Later, it is hard to recall exactly what happened and the feedback loses its impact.

By invitation

The best feedback is feedback that is asked for: 'How did I do?', 'What do you think I should do to improve?'.

If you are asked, give honest, supportive, constructive feedback.

Share the effect

It might help the receiver to know the results of their behaviour; for example, its effects on you, a customer, or a performance goal.

Follow the KISS principle

Keep It Short And Sincere.

Feedback is a powerful management tool. Use it to build relationships and good performance.

Put yourself on the same wavelength

15

Have you ever worked with someone who irritates you? Or someone you just don't seem to be on the same wavelength with? You're 'out of rapport' with these people and because of this, it's difficult to communicate well with them.

Rapport (pronounced *ra-pore*) is essential to effective communication. It is the feeling of being *in synch* or *in harmony* with another person. When we're 'in rapport' with someone, we feel comfortable with them and communication flows.

In this chapter we see how an understanding of personality types and temperaments can help you put

Use terms and language people can understand and alter your vocabulary to suit the person and the situation. Talk in the other person's 'language'.

yourself on the same wavelength as another person and how to communicate with them in a way that they can readily relate to. In Chapter 25 we find out how to build and test rapport through body language.

Our choice of words is important and how we can choose words to match the other person's preferred representational system (visual, auditory, kinaesthetic, or digital) was discussed in Chapter 10.

Find out people's main needs

We can divide people's main psychological needs into three common groups: need for achievement, need for affiliation, and need for power. Recognising and directing your communications towards these needs also helps build rapport.

People with a high **need for achievement** are those who set specific, measurable goals and standards and keep working until they've accomplished them. They always want to do it better—perhaps better than they've done it before, perhaps better than anyone has ever done it, perhaps to push the current standard further out.

Allow these people to take responsibility for their own performance and make sure they receive plenty of feedback on how well they're doing.

'Never say die' and 'Where's the next challenge?' seem to be their mottoes. Their satisfaction comes from accomplishing goals efficiently.

> Who does this sound like to you? List them below:
>
> _____ _____ _____

Other people are more interested in friendly, cordial, working relationships. What pleases them is working with others whose company they enjoy in an easy, give-and-take, relaxed atmosphere. Their high **need for affiliation** drives them, for example, to write more letters, spend more time with their co-workers, talk on the phone more, and they prefer to work with friends rather than strangers.

Take care to establish friendly working relationships with people who have a high need for affiliation. Ask about their family, their weekends, their outside-of-work interests, how they think and feel about things.

> Who does this sound like to you? List them below:
>
> _____   _____   _____

Others thrive on taking charge. Such people have a high **need for power**. They aim for authority so that they can decide what should be done and make it happen. They surround themselves with prestigious possessions as symbols of their power, communicate assertively, and are able to influence others in most communication situations.

When dealing with people who need power, allow them to feel in charge; recognise their need to be treated as powerful and important.

> Who does this sound like to you? List them below:
>
> _____   _____   _____

Since we're each unique, we each have a different 'need recipe'; we each have varying mixes and strengths of the needs for achievement, affiliation, and power.

Listen to the main themes underlying what people say. What pleases them? Achievement—completing things efficiently, beating their own records, accomplishing goals? Affiliation—genial working relationships, making friends of people, helping them? Power—being consulted and listened to, taking charge, making things happen? When you know what drives people, you'll know how to tailor your communications to fit in with their needs.

Take personality into account

People are complex. Nevertheless it is helpful to learn reliable ways of spotting fundamental personality differences and how to cope with them.

Since the pioneering work of Dr Carl Jung in the field of personality types, psychologists have expanded greatly on his findings.

He distinguished between **introverts**, who make up 25 per cent of the population and are most interested in the inner world of concepts and ideas; and **extroverts**, the other 75 per cent who relate best to the external world of people and things. Introverts are reflective while extroverts are action-oriented. It is often said that introverts think before they speak and extroverts speak before they think.

Find out what ideas are important to introverts and try and fit your communications into their idea framework.

Show extroverts how what you are saying fits in with other people's thinking and what the rest of the world is doing.

Then there is a **task focus** or a **people focus**. Some people focus on the task at hand, on finishing the job, while others focus more on the people: does everyone understand and agree with our objectives? Is everyone satisfied, comfortable, happy?

Focus on the task at hand when holding discussions with task-oriented people. Include discussion on people issues when talking with people-oriented people.

Four preferences for dealing with information

Jung also described fundamental differences in the way we perceive and process information and what we do with it. He found that we receive and process information by four methods: thinking, feeling, intuiting, and sensing.

Most of us prefer to use one of these four methods, but we can use another one or two if we need to, and we have one method that is underdeveloped and seldom used.

Thinkers, as you might guess, are strong on clear, logical thinking. They are methodical and good at analysing problems. They are good with facts and figures, researching, and systems analysis.

Who do you know like this? List them below:

_____   _____   _____

Help thinkers by stating the overall theory or concept of what you are presenting. Give them information in a logical built-up sequence. Deal with facts impersonally and consistently.

Feelers see things through their personal values and their judgments are based on these, rather than on an objective weighing up of pros and cons. They are warm and outgoing and enjoy being with people. They excel in cementing team relationships, counselling, arbitrating, and public relations.

Make your values explicit with feelers so they can feel 'where you're coming from'. Take care that they feel supported and not threatened by you.

Who do you know like this? List them below:

_____   _____   _____

Intuitors have fertile imaginations and provide creative ideas. They work from intuition and hunches and with possibilities, and are good at long-term planning, creative writing, and generating ideas.

Who do you know like this? List them below:

_____   _____   _____

Give intuitors an idea of where you're headed, of what your visions and ultimate goals are. Then let their creative minds work out how to help you achieve those ends.

Sensors are down-to-earth people, energetic, and practical. They prefer action to words and ideas and like to get on with it. They deal in the here-and-now. They're best at initiating projects, setting up deals, negotiating, troubleshooting, and converting ideas into action.

Who do you know like this? List them below:

_____   _____   _____

Don't embellish things with too much detail or fancy theory for sensors. Communicate clearly, to the point, and in practical terms and results.

Four types of people

Katharine Myers and Isabel Briggs researched personality types and, drawing from Jung's works, distinguished 16 personality types. These are based on a person's preferences for dealing with people and information.

Here we group these 16 types into two sets of four main groups. This makes it easier to spot important differences between people and communicate better with them.

Combining the introversion–extroversion and task–people continuums discussed above gives us the first of the two main groups of four different personality types: dominant directors, interacting socialisers, steady relaters, and conscientious thinkers.

Dominant directors

These are extroverts who focus on the task. They are outgoing, direct, competitive, and results-oriented. They use their initiative, are willing to confront people, make decisions easily, and are often ambitious. They have a strong need for power, enjoy taking charge and resist authority from others.

Often considered 'blunt', dominant directors get to the point quickly. They're fast-paced and want things done *now*. They dislike sloppy results.

Who do you know like this? List them below:

_____   _____   _____

Treat dominant directors with all the respect they think they deserve. Let them think they're in charge. Don't question their authority.

Present good work and communicate accurately, clearly, and to the point with the dominant directors you work with. Don't try their patience with abstract conceptualisations which they would see as lacking substance, or with a lot of focus on people issues which they would see as insufficiently businesslike. Keep your eye on the ball: stay focused on the 'bottom line' and results.

Interacting socialisers

These people are extroverts who focus on people issues. They like people and their needs revolve around affiliation. They are outgoing, sociable, talkative, persuasive, and impulsive. Often disorganised and inattentive to detail, they are good at influencing others. They can't sit still, are fun-loving and energetic, creative, and open with their feelings. They thrive on change, new trends and ideas, and recognition of their achievement.

Who do you know like this? List them below:

_____   _____   _____

Keep details and detailed work well away from interacting socialisers or they feel confined. Let them talk, participate, motivate, and create an enjoyable atmosphere. Treat them as friends.

Steady relaters

Steady relaters are introverts who are concerned with people and affiliation more than the task. They dislike conflict. They prefer a known and stable routine to the untried and untested. Quiet and often unassertive, they are stable, consistent, valuable and easy-going team players, helpful and eager to please. Good thinkers and patient listeners, steady relaters are good at calming down upset people. They are the glue that hold work teams together.

Who do you know like this? List them below:

_____   _____   _____

If you want to find out what a steady relater's thoughts or opinions are, you may have to ask many open questions and listen carefully; it will be worth it. Make sure you don't overlook them or take their loyalty and contributions for granted.

Conscientious thinkers

Conscientious thinkers are orderly and systematic. They are introverts who have a strong need for achievement and who focus on the task. They enjoy study and analysis and approach projects and tasks in a deliberate, objective and thorough fashion. They are accurate, well-organised, have high standards and produce high-quality work.

Who do you know like this? List them below:

_____   _____   _____

I'D BETTER RE-CHECK THAT!

Don't ask conscientious thinkers to turn in rushed 'close enough is good enough' jobs and don't *ever* present any to them! If you need to criticise, do so gently. Explain things fully and carefully and don't forget the details that they crave. If changes are required, don't rush it; spell them out clearly and give them time to ask questions and adjust to the changes.

Four temperaments

The next set of four personality groupings is: analyst, legalist, realist, and empathist. These also highlight important differences between people and help us to communicate with them better.

Analysts

Analysts make up only 12 per cent of the population and are valuable for their creativity and good ideas. They're serious, competent, competitive self-starters who are often said to be married to their job; work is the focus of their life. They are conceptual, theoretical, logical thinkers who work best on their own.

Keep detail, routine and practical matters away from analysts. Tell them what you want and then give them the chance to develop the plan. Give them ways of keeping score and ask for their thoughts, especially when you are short on good ideas.

Legalists

Legalists are conservative, serious, loyal, responsible, steady, accurate, and practical. They tend also to be cautious, seek security, and avoid change. They make up 40 per cent of the population and are good at working with details. They work best in structured, predictable situations.

Provide structured, hands-on training to legalists and make sure they understand the structure and systems they work with; count on them to follow the regulations and keep to the routines.

Provide them with the detail they need to complete their work and with formal tokens of recognition for their contributions and efforts. Be punctual and thorough when dealing with legalists and don't spring any surprises on them. They will resist change, so explain any required changes fully and carefully to them.

Realists

Realists make up about 35 per cent of the population. They're the technical, hands-on, practical people, the 'can-do', action-oriented trouble-shooter. Often flamboyant, spontaneous, impulsive and fun-loving, they thrive on excitement. They're open-minded, tolerant, flexible, and good at coping with change.

Give realists hands-on training and help with their self-organisation and time management. Give them plenty of freedom and enough variety so they don't get bored. Help them perfect their skills. Count on them to rise to the challenge in a crisis. Enjoy their company.

Empathists

Empathists are helpers, supporters, and encouragers. They are the warm, spiritual, and communicative 13 per cent of the population. They work towards harmony and for meaning.

Give empathists personal instruction and encouragement. Make sure they know the importance of the job they're doing. Appreciate their contributions and if you find it necessary to offer negative feedback, do it carefully so that it isn't interpreted as a personal attack. Give empathists autonomy and a chance to learn. Don't burden them with detail.

In each of these two groupings of four personality types or temperaments no one of the four is any better or worse than any other—each is different and valuable in its own way.

As managers, it is important to recognise and work with peoples' strengths; these groupings can help you do this. Recognising key differences between people will also help you to communicate better.

Differences among people are great. These differences make life interesting and help us achieve. After all: *If both of us thought the same, one of us would be unnecessary.*

PART III

Gathering good
information

Learning how things are
from the other person's
point of view

PART III

Focus on the speaker

16

Failure to focus attentively on the speaker is at the root of many communication difficulties. How often do you tune someone out as disturbing 'background noise'? While this might, at times, be desirable with a three-year-old's continuous chatter, 'tuning out' short-circuits any chance of good communication with adults.

How often have you pretended to listen while continuing what you were doing or thinking? Appearing to give the speaker our attention and occasionally nodding our head and mumbling 'uh-huh' is not communication.

How often have you listened with only half an ear, intending to 'tune in' when something of significance is said? Unfortunately, our ability to filter information selectively in this way is not very good and a great deal of valuable information goes unheard as a result.

There are many other bad habits that obstruct focusing on the speaker. Are any of these yours?

Ask yourself, do I:

- formulate my own reply while the other person speaks?
- let my mind wander?
- 'tune out' a point of view that differs from my own preconceived ideas?
- interrupt speakers?
- finish speakers' sentences for them?
- talk while other people are speaking?
- jump to conclusions?
- hear only what I want to hear, expect to hear, or what I assume the speaker will say?

Yet the truth is, people speaking often need to feel heard before they can hear. Gathering good information must often precede giving good information.

The first step to gathering good information is to focus on the speaker. Not *pretend* to focus, but genuinely attend to what the speaker is saying, feeling, and meaning. We do this with our eyes, our ears, and our hearts.

We need to see things from the speaker's point of view before we can truly understand it. This will help us to develop empathy for and understanding of the speaker and to respond appropriately.

More than that, the speaker needs to *sense* that we are trying to understand their point of view and that we won't ignore it, stifle it, criticise or condemn it. Only then will the speaker feel able to continue giving us good information.

Gathering good information hinges on being able to focus on the speaker. If you are too busy or preoccupied to do this, arrange a better time to meet.

There are many things you can do to improve your ability to focus on the speaker. These can be grouped under environmental, physical, mental, and verbal actions.

Is the environment right?

As discussed in Chapter 3, it is important to remove anything that hinders you from focusing on the speaker. Noise and other distractions stop you from attending and these block the communication process.

Attend physically

Attend physically, too.

> Make eye contact, sit openly (do not cross your arms or legs) and face the speaker. Nod and make comments to show that you are following the speaker's train of thought. Lean slightly towards the speaker to show interest.

This helps you focus on the speaker and encourages the speaker to give you more information because they can see that they have your attention.

Attend mentally

If something else is on your mind, put it mentally to one side for now (or note it down if you think you might forget it); it will still be there when you've finished.

Follow the speaker's train of thought. If the topic is very important, you may even want to take notes to help keep the information straight in your mind and help you concentrate. Certainly, you will want to summarise the main points mentally as you listen and note any shifts in the speaker's body language, tone of voice, facial expression, and so on.

Listen to understand, not evaluate.

Suspend judgment. If you are assessing the worth,

accuracy or validity of what is being said as you listen, you'll commit some of the 11 deadly communication sins described in Chapter 8.

Pay attention to the representational system in which the other person is speaking (Chapter 10); listen to discover the motives and personality type or temperament (Chapter 15). Listen for the meanings behind the words: what is *really* being said? What else is needed from you? What can be done so that your point of view is understood?

Check it

If you're not sure you've heard or understood something correctly, check it.

Give yourself time to think. Don't feel you need to respond the moment the speaker pauses. Reflect on what has been said and its meaning. Then perhaps restate it to check your understanding.

The speaker will see this thoughtfulness as an indication that you care about what has been said and you care about what you are going to say.

Focusing on the speaker is the first and perhaps most important step in gathering good information. It helps you to:

- give the speaker time to have their say
- let the speaker finish without interrupting
- stick to the point
- give non-verbal signals that you are listening (nodding, 'uh-huhs', eye contact)
- act and respond appropriately
- remember what was said
- avoid being side-tracked or distracted.

And it helps the speaker to feel comfortable with you.

Whenever good communication is important, whenever there is a need to gather and to give good information, focus on the speaker. If you sense that someone is resisting what you're saying, disagrees, or is confused or uncertain, it is even more important to *really* focus on them and find out what is going on for them.

Gather some good information. Ask what is worrying, troubling, concerning or confusing them; what is holding them back from agreeing or giving you their full support? What other information do they need? The more fully you can focus on them and what they're saying, the more information you will gather. And the more difficult the communication situation is, the more you will need this information.

Listen, listen, listen

Gathering good information is more than just hearing. It has to do with the quality of your listening: the responses you make, the questions you ask, and your body language.

Listening is a gift you can give.

If a speaker's message, or your relationship with the speaker is important, don't just *hear* what is said—really *listen*. Listening is more than the other half of speaking. True listening is done with your heart and eyes as well as your ears.

True listening requires us to temporarily set aside our own thoughts, expectations, biases, and desires. Only then can we fully concentrate on what is being said and experience the world from the speaker's point of view.

145

This is hard work. When you *really* listen, your blood pressure rises, your temperature goes up, and your pulse increases. These are the same physiological changes that would occur if you stepped outside to dig a trench.

The intention to listen is not enough. Would you let your mother give you heart surgery? Probably not unless she were a heart surgeon. Good intention without skills is luck.

Listening is a sophisticated skill requiring considerable practice. There are, after all, many bad habits to overcome, and because listening is hard work, it's so much easier *not* to really listen . . .

Why don't we listen better?

There are many reasons. Here are some:

- We think we have something better to say ourselves.
- We're given no reason to listen.
- We think we know what they'll say.
- There are too many distractions.
- We don't like the speaker or the message.
- Our minds are closed.
- We hear what we want to hear.
- We jump to conclusions.
- We'd rather be talking—we feel more active and more in control.
- We let our minds wander.
- We listen only for where we can break in to speak.

The ability to listen is an important management skill. It is probably the most under-rated skill in communication. Yet listening is essential in order to gather and give good information. It breaks down communication barriers, filters, and incompatibilities. Listening is important in establishing and maintaining good relationships and avoiding conflict and misunderstandings. Ask anyone who works well with others what their secret is, and 90 per cent of them are likely to give you an answer that involves the ability to listen.

How can we listen? Let us count the ways . . .

There are many levels of listening, ranging from tuning someone out and not listening, to listening actively and with empathy.

'Half-an-ear' listening

Many forms of 'listening' are actually unhelpful. Listening with half an ear, for example, shows itself in our body language and discourages all but the most determined speaker.

'Stunned mullet' listening

'Stunned mullet' listening, or listening passively (blank stares, no non-verbal signals to encourage the speaker) may be fine for watching television but it discourages a speaker from continuing, and actually makes it quite difficult to do so.

'Acknowledgment' listening

We can gather twice as much information from 'acknowledgment' listening. When we nod and grunt while the other speaks, it shows them we are following their thoughts. It encourages them to continue without disrupting their flow. The main drawback with acknowledgment listening is that there is no feedback to check our understanding.

Active listening

Active listening is the highest level of listening. The most difficult in terms of skills and effort required, it brings us the greatest rewards in information, understanding, and results. Accurate communication is more likely to occur with active listening than with any other form of listening.

Active listening stimulates thought in both the speaker and the listener and keeps both communicators actively involved in the conversation. First, it requires the listener to do some mental work to understand what the speaker is saying. This understanding is then fed back to the speaker, allowing the listener to check understanding.

Second, an active listening response can help the speaker to clarify thoughts and communicate these more accurately. Words and often thoughts are imprecise and people seldom *say* what they *mean*. An active listening response helps the speaker to develop thoughts and gives them a chance to clarify what has been said or add further information. With active listening you gather more good information than from any other form of listening. It makes the communication dance far more satisfying.

The message that active listening sends is: 'I want to hear and understand everything you have to say'.

With active listening, we need to use our eyes, too, and take the speaker's body language into account.

Notice that you can feed back your understanding of either the *meaning* of what the speaker has said, or their *feelings* about it. Do whichever suits the occasion and the context of your conversation.

Take what you have seen and heard, mentally summarise it, and then restate, in your own words, the speaker's main points or how you understand the speaker to be feeling.

Notice, too, that an active listening response doesn't necessarily suggest agreement. You may agree with, feel ambivalent about, or strongly disagree with the speaker. However, even if you disagree, you can still give an active listening response to show you have listened to, and understood, the speaker's point of view.

Make sure you summarise your understanding in a tentative, not dogmatic way.

The speaker may want to modify your active listening restatement; this is fine—it just means you haven't understood perfectly.

If what you have said is precisely what the speaker meant, further clarification or more information will probably follow. Either way, you're learning a great deal about the speaker's thoughts and feelings.

Once you've given your active listening response, allow the speaker a moment to consider what you've said before replying.

When several points are made, summarise the one that you want to focus on. This will help you keep the conversation pointed in the direction you want to take.

Keep your active listening restatement short to keep the focus on the speaker.

When several emotions are expressed, reflect the final one; this is usually the most accurate.

Only reflect what's there—don't start guessing.

Summarise your understanding in a tentative way

'You sound . . .'
'You seem . . .'
'Your idea is . . .'
'To you it must be like . . .'
'That must irritate you.'
'Let me summarise . . .'
'You seem to be saying . . .'
'You must feel as though . . .'
'If I understand you correctly . . .'

These are statements. This is because a question could get only a 'yes' or 'no' reply, or a reply at a more superficial level. Active listening statements encourage an accurate and complete reply.

Wait out thoughtful silences.

Because active listening requires so much effort, you may not want to do it all the time. Use your active listening skills in the following situations:

When to use active listening

To draw out information

- to draw out more information
- to show the speaker you are listening and to encourage them to continue
- when encountering new ideas
- when there's a problem to be solved and you need to gather all the facts
- to draw out the full story
- when you're not sure what the speaker means.

When there is conflict

- whenever you think you disagree with the speaker
- before you argue or criticise.

To affirm or support someone

- when the speaker wants to talk
- immediately after making an 'I' statement.

In emotional situations

- to calm down an upset, angry, or otherwise emotional person
- when a speaker has said something with real emotion in their voice
- if the speaker is talking about a personal matter or problem
- if the speaker is talking about their feelings and emotions.

Don't make active listening statements when you are unable to accept and respect the speaker. You might use emotive words or phrases and/or a critical tone of voice, which would warn the speaker to stop rather than encourage them to continue.

And don't use active listening as a substitute for assertion or a way of hiding yourself, your own thoughts or your own feelings.

Remain neutral. It's better to show neither disapproval nor approval when giving an active listening response.

Five active listening skills

Paraphrasing

This involves translating into your own words what the speaker has said, to check your understanding.

Speaker:	*'. . . and I find it so frustrating because I'm really doing my best to get the project finished on time. I'm quite happy to put in the extra hours it takes, but everything and everyone seem against me!'*
Active listening response:	*'You sound as if you feel let down and that you're not getting enough support.'*
Speaker:	*'Yes, that's just it, and . . .'*

Reflecting feelings

When someone is expressing emotion or feelings or looks emotional (upset, angry, excited), convey your empathy.

Speaker:	*'I'm so fed up! How do they expect me to manage properly when the budgets come out with so many inaccuracies. I spend most of my time poring over them to spot the mistakes instead of doing my job!'*
Active listening response:	*'That certainly sounds annoying.'*
Speaker:	*'You're not kidding! The point is, there's so much to get done and I need to be hampered like this like I need a hole in my head.'*
Active listening response:	*'You sound really fed up.'*
Speaker:	*'I suppose I am. . . Really, what I'd like is . . .'*

Speaker:	*'This sales increase project is going nowhere except around in circles!'*
Active listening response:	*'You sound pretty frustrated.'*
Speaker:	*'Yes, I am. It's all talk and no action. We can't even agree on the basic principles. Still, I guess it's early days yet.'*

Reflecting meanings

Briefly summarise the content, or factual aspects, of what the speaker has said.

Speaker:	*'There's been a lot of activity while you were away. Angie crashed her car and needed a few days off. Bernie came down with the flu; Kerry sprained her ankle, and we had to get a temp who somehow managed to lose all our main files off the master disk. I'm really glad you're back!'*
Active listening response:	*'Well! It sounds as though you've had plenty to keep you busy all right!'*
Speaker:	*'I'll say! And if I do say so myself, I think I managed everything quite well. Here's what I've done . . .'*

Synthesising

Blend several ideas of the speaker into one theme or idea.

Speaker:	*'. . . The first thing that happened was a major policy change, which no-one could possibly have predicted. Then one of our best technicians resigned. Then the deadline was brought forward; I suppose we could have seen that coming. It's been one thing after another.'*
Active listening response:	*'So there's been a series of stumbling blocks making this a particularly difficult project.'*
Speaker:	*'You're not kidding! I think the straw that broke the camel's back was the policy change. If it weren't for that we'd have a fighting chance.'*
Active listening response:	*'You sound as if you feel all is lost.'*
Speaker:	*'Well, not **all** lost. We're certainly behind the eight ball, though.'*

Imagining aloud

Imagine what it must be like to be in the speaker's place.

Manager:	*'. . . and so I really need those reports to be finished on time in future.'*

Employee:	*'I just can't seem to satisfy anybody around here! Everyone's my boss; everyone complains. If it isn't one thing it's another.'*
Manager:	*'It guess it must be hard for you.'*
Employee:	*'It's just that . . .'*

Speaker:	*'. . . and I really don't know which way to jump. There are pros and cons to each action and the repercussions could be quite serious.'*
Active listening response:	*'If I were in your place, I think I'd feel rather hesitant to make any decision in case I made the wrong one.'*
Speaker:	*'Yes, that's just it . . . I guess I really need some more information . . . Perhaps I'll gather a few opinions, too, from people who have more experience in this area than I do.'*

When do you stop active listening? Whenever you feel the speaker has said all there is to say; when the full story has been heard.

Then move to the obvious next step. This may be, for example, problem-solving, saying how you see things from your point of view, or deciding what should happen next.

With practice, your skills at listening will improve. But true listening is never effortless and always requires a degree of self-discipline.

The results are worth the effort. After all, no-one is likely to do you the honour of listening to you if you don't do them the honour of listening to them.

Draw out the full story

18

Seeing things from the speaker's point of view is essential for good communication. We have looked at the importance of focusing on the speaker and listening, with hearts and eyes as well as ears, to the real message behind the words. In this chapter we look at a four-step formula for drawing out the full story.

Four steps to the full story

Step 1 Ask an open question

If you ask a closed question, chances are you receive the least information; people usually respond with a 'Yes', a 'No', or a fact.

Closed questions	
'What is your favourite animal?'	*'A dog.'*
'Do you like your job?'	*'Yes.'*
'Did you have any problems?'	*'No.'*
'Who do you work for?'	*'John.'*

Closed questions are good for finding out facts and for preventing someone from being longwinded. They are not helpful for drawing out the full story, though.

To draw out the full story use open questions. An open question is any question that encourages the speaker to provide fuller information and details.

Open questions

'Tell me about your favourite animal.'

'What do you like most about your work?'

'What problems did you run into?'

'What's your boss like?'

Note that some open questions are statements. Note also that there is no real rule, such as 'Open questions start with who, what, where, when, why, how'; that is not always true.

Asking open questions needs more skill than most people realise. So here's some practice. Rephrase these closed questions to make them open. There are a few ideas in Appendix 3.

'When did that happen?'   _____

'Was your trip successful?'   _____

'Did you like that candidate?'   _____

'Did you have a good meeting?' _____

'Why did that happen?'   _____

Try to avoid questions that start with 'Why . . .', like 'Why did you do that?' People can be made defensive by such questions, and unwilling to give you the information you need.

Step 2 Affirm

While the speaker is talking, use acknowledgment listening techniques to show you're listening and to encourage them to continue. In other words, nod and grunt and use attentive body language.

Step 3 Restate

Now give an active listening response. Restate, in your own words, the gist of what the speaker has expressed— either as feelings or meanings, whichever you decide is more appropriate.

This allows you to check your understanding and allows the speaker to clear up any misunderstandings. It also helps you to draw out the full story, since an active listening response is invariably followed by more information and elaboration.

Step 4 Silence

When you have given the active listening response: pause; allow the speaker time to think about what you have said and how to respond. Because active listening responses stimulate well-considered replies, this may take a few seconds, so be patient.

And that's all there is to it. Recycle step 1 through step 4 and step 2 through step 4 as often as necessary to draw out the full story. Then, when you present your point of view it will be based on a thorough understanding of the speaker's point of view.

THE FULL STORY

SILENCE

RESTATE

AFFIRM

OPEN QUESTION

Appendix 3
Closed to open questions

Your ideas will probably be different, so these are just suggestions.

To test whether you have succeeded in turning the closed questions into open questions, ask yourself whether you could answer your reworded question with a simple 'yes', 'no', or a short statement of fact; if you can, they are still closed questions.

When did that happen?	*What led up to that?*
Was your trip successful?	*What did you manage to accomplish on your trip?*
Did you like that candidate?	*In what ways do you think that candidate meets our needs?*
Did you have a good meeting?	*What happened at the meeting?*
Why did that happen?	*What could have caused that?*

Ask the right questions

19

Sometimes people need help to give us good information. When this happens, we can ask questions to draw out the full story, to fill out the details, to form a clear picture. Questions can also determine a speaker's frame of reference, wants, needs, hopes and fears.

Avoid unhelpful questions

Asking questions is a bit of an art. In Chapter 11 we saw the dangers of asking pseudo questions. In Chapter 18 we saw that closed questions are not helpful for drawing out good information and that 'Why . . .' questions can make people defensive. Let's run through some other unhelpful questions.

To pseudo questions, closed questions, and 'Why. . .' questions, we can add leading questions and multiple questions to complete the list of unhelpful kinds of questions.

Leading questions

A leading question implies the answer you are looking for; the person you address it to would have to be brave, stupid, or reckless to give you the 'wrong' answer.

- An interviewer might ask a job candidate: 'Would you accept this job if it were offered to you?'
- A manager might ask a team member: 'You won't have problems with that, will you?'
- Someone might ask their partner: 'How do you like the meal I've prepared, dear?'

WHO LOVES YOU MORE, MUMMY OR DADDY?

Multiple questions

A **multiple question** is several questions within one question. These confuse people because they don't know which one to answer first and usually answer only the last one. Unfortunately, as we add to the string of questions, each one tends to be more trite and meaningless than the last, so we finish up with very little information.

- A manager might ask a team member: 'How did you get on with that? Did you have any troubles? Anything you'd like to tell me about? Anything at all? Or was everything all right?'
- Someone might ask a co-worker: 'Do you think I should accept the transfer to your section? What's it like working there? Is everyone friendly? Is the supervisor nice? Are they sticklers for timekeeping or is everything fairly relaxed? Do you think I should transfer?'
- A manager might ask an employee: 'I'm worried because you've seemed a bit quiet and despondent

lately. I wondered if there was a problem at home, perhaps. Or perhaps you've cleared everything up? Or maybe there's a work problem you'd like to talk to me about? Or is it just that you're feeling a bit quiet lately?'

As you can see, multiple questions won't be of much help in drawing out good information.

Question neutrally

If we want to find out information, opinions, or even facts, we'll need to ask in an unprovocative, neutral tone of voice. The other person first has to feel sufficiently relaxed to be willing and able to give us the information we need.

A neutral tone of voice, used with the following information, will help you to avoid costly and embarrassing miscommunications and misunderstandings. You will be able to clear up ambiguities and draw out the full story.

Use general, probing, and unspoken questions

General questions

A general question is good for introducing a topic or highlighting the one you wish to pursue further.

'Jan, you just mentioned the difficulties you've had with the ticketing procedure. Can you tell me a bit more about them?'

Probing questions

Probing questions are those that follow along the topic you want to explore further.

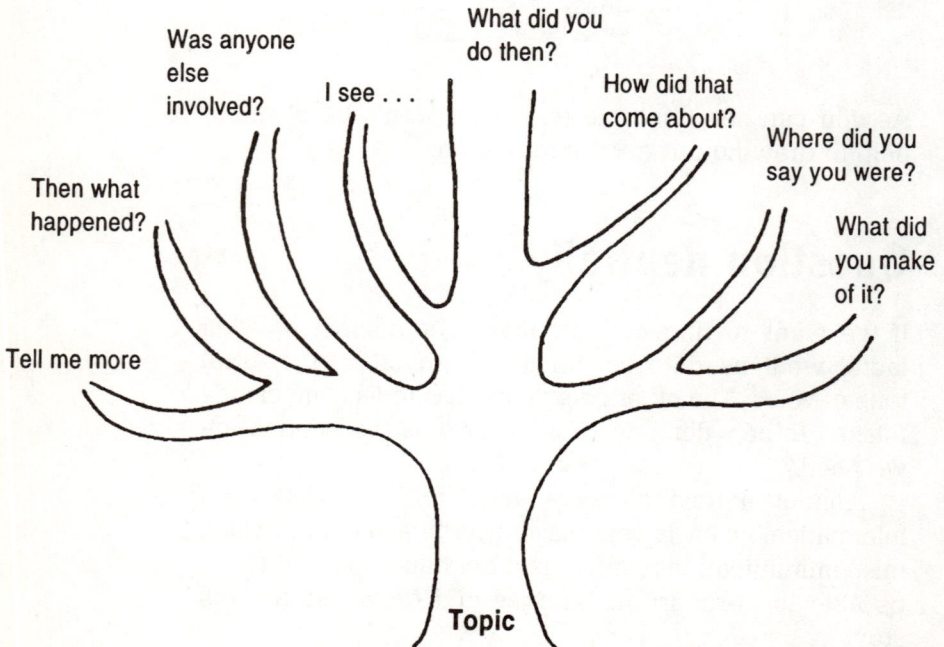

Was anyone else involved?

What did you do then?

I see . . .

How did that come about?

Where did you say you were?

Then what happened?

What did you make of it?

Tell me more

Topic

Unspoken questions

Unspoken questions are asked non-verbally: the raised eyebrow, the expectant pause, the 'Hmmm?' with a rising inflection. These encourage most people to continue.

Help people to be specific

When someone makes a vague statement such as:

'That's not good enough.'

'That's not acceptable to me.'

'He's very rich.'

'She's completely undependable!'

you can help them to become more specific by asking, in effect, 'What [vague word] specifically?' Your goal is to help the other person make their communication more clear and concrete. Otherwise, you won't ever know for sure what they're talking about.

For example:

'That's not good enough.'

> *'I'm not clear about just what you mean by "not good enough"; what would help to make it good enough?'* or *'In what way is it not good enough?'*

'That's not acceptable to me.'

> *'What would make it acceptable to you?'* or
> *'Can you give me an idea of what in particular isn't acceptable to you?'*

'He's very rich.'

> *'How rich?'*

'She's completely undependable!'

> *'In what ways is she undependable?'*

Help make assumptions and 'rules' explicit

Words like 'should', 'shouldn't', 'must', 'have to', 'can't', and 'ought' imply an underlying assumption or an unstated rule. It is often very useful to bring assumptions and unspoken 'rules' into the open and test them against reality. This can be done by asking a question.

Merely repeating the word or phrase in a questioning tone can often encourage the speaker to clarify the statement. *'Should?'*, *'Shouldn't?'*, *'You must?'*, *'You feel you ought to?'* Or you might say: *'What would happen if you did/didn't?'*

Depending on the situation, you might need to soften

these questions with modifiers like: 'I wonder what would happen if you didn't . . .' or 'I'm curious about what you mean by . . .'

You might also need to take special care to build rapport non-verbally (see Chapter 24); otherwise, these questions, while bringing assumptions and 'rules' to the surface, might also be interpreted as challenging them.

Help tie down universals

One of the functions of the brain is to make the complicated and often contradictory processes of life nice and tidy. This helps us to go through each day without too much trauma, and in a reasonably efficient manner.

In the processes of tidying-up we devise universals, or generalise from one or a few similar situations to all similar situations.

For example, if you work for an authoritarian and inconsiderate boss, you might conclude that that is how all bosses are. If you have a run of bad luck with a few team members, you may generalise that all team members are lazy, irresponsible and undependable. If you have been 'dropped in it' once by the production manager, you may conclude that all production managers must be watched carefully.

Just as assumptions and unstated rules often benefit from exposure and examination, so too do universals. Clues to universals are words that make generalisations, such as 'always', 'never', 'all', and 'every'. Again, questions such as 'Always?', 'Never?', 'What would happen if you did?' can be asked. This will provide new information.

Similarly, we can ask questions to find out what's behind ambiguous words such as 'they', as in 'They won't allow that'. Questions such as 'Who won't allow that?' or 'What would happen if we did it anyway?' will usually provide you with more good information.

Help analyse comparisons

Many comparisons are made every day. Words like 'better', 'worse', 'easier', 'harder' and so on, will alert you to the need to make the comparison explicit so that you can assess its validity. This also uncovers a lot of useful information.

'He's the best man for the job' could lead you to ask, for example: 'Better than whom?' or 'Better than which other men?' or even 'Surely not better than a woman?!'

'Better than what?', 'Worse than what?', 'Easier than what?' will be the theme of the questions you ask here to make the comparisons more explicit and help you to test them.

Avoid interrogating

Sometimes you need to gather a lot of information quickly. This can lead you to ask a string of closed questions. Suppose, for example, you go into a tyre store to buy a new set of tyres. The salesperson will need to know your driving habits in order to recommend the appropriate tyre for your needs. Information such as how many kilometres a year you drive, the kind of roads you drive on and the loads that you normally carry must all be considered, along with your driving habits and main concerns as a driver.

Imagine a conversation like this:

Salesperson: *'How much driving do you do?'*

Customer: *'Oh, I'd say in the region of about 300 to 350 kilometres a week.'*

Salesperson: *'What sort of roads?'*

Customer: *'Uhm, mostly tarmac; the odd dirt track at weekends.'*

Salesperson:	*'Speeds?'*
Customer:	*'Oh, I'm pretty law-abiding.'*
Salesperson:	*'What do you carry?'*
Customer:	*'Just granny and the kids at the weekend. Otherwise, it's just me.'*

Our salesperson has some information. Now suppose the salesperson softens each question by preceding it with a short summary of what the customer has just said. This shows the customer that he or she is being listened to, and makes the discussion more like a relaxed, friendly conversation.

Salesperson:	*'How much driving would you say you do?'*
Customer:	*'Oh, I'd say in the region of about 300 to 350 kilometres a week.'*
Salesperson:	*'I see; fairly average mileage there. And what sort of roads do you mostly drive on?'*
Customer:	*'Uhm, mostly tarmac; the odd dirt track at weekends, though, but not often.'*
Salesperson:	*'OK, so pretty good roads, usually.'*
Customer:	*'Well, actually, I go up and down into the hills nearly every day.'*
Salesperson:	*'I see. That actually adds a lot of wear to your tyres. I suppose cornering and handling are important to you?'*
Customer:	*'Oh, absolutely.'*
Salesperson:	*'And what sort of speeds do you normally drive at?'*
Customer:	*'Oh, I'm pretty law-abiding. I generally keep to the speed limit.'*

Salesperson: *'OK, so we don't need a super high performance tyre. Do you carry any loads at all?'*

Customer: *'Just granny and the kids at the weekend. Otherwise, it's just me.'*

There's a lot more information for the salesperson to work from here. In addition, we have a customer who is feeling much more relaxed and disposed towards making a purchase.

To stop a series of fact-finding questions becoming an interrogation, make a short summary of each answer before you ask your next question.

Use questions to check if your message has been understood

Questions can also help us make sure that the other person has understood our message. You may want to ask someone you have just given some instructions to how they plan to proceed; this will show you whether you've communicated clearly. Or you may want to ask a person to summarise for you their understanding of what has just been agreed, to highlight any areas of misunderstanding that need to be cleared up.

However you choose to ask, your aim is to be sure that clear communication has taken place before you say your 'goodbyes'. This will save many problems and embarrassment later on.

Make it a habit to ask questions to draw out good information. It will save you time and frustration.

PART IV

Watch that body language!

Improving communication through body language

Basic principles of body language

20

> SHOOT! I CAN'T FIDGET WITH A SHIRT CUFF. WE HAVEN'T INVENTED IT YET!

Although some people are better at reading body language than others, we're all quite expert at it. In fact, we do it every day, usually unconsciously. Quickly, in the blink of an eye, we sense whether a person is friendly or sure of themselves or trustworthy or truthful.

This is as it should be. Spontaneous and automatic application of a skill implies proficiency. And as body language accounts for about 65 per cent of any spoken message, it is a useful language to master.

By becoming aware of some basic elements of body language we can enhance our communications with others. We can make sure that the body language signals we send out to others are relaying the messages we intend. We can more easily encourage others to communicate with us.

We can recognise more readily problems such as lack of understanding, disagreement, or budding conflict. We can pick up early signals of support, agreement or encouragement. We can improve our timing and gauge when to speak up and when not to, when to press for agreement and when to bide our time, when to lighten up and when to apply pressure.

The body speaks on levels that are often unconscious. Like any other form of communication, it is not a sure means of transmitting a message from one person to another, but it is often more revealing than verbal language. Our communications can become more effective by taking our own, and other people's, body language into account.

Your own body language starts from the inside

21

At the core of our success is the view we hold about ourselves—our self-esteem and self-image. Everything we do and say flows from these.

Self-esteem

What is self-esteem? It involves the value we place on ourselves as people and the expectations we have of ourselves. It is how comfortable we are with who we are.

How high is your self-esteem?

Do you:

	5	4	3	2	1	
Act with confidence?						Act with little confidence?
Make your own decisions?						Let others make them for you?
Look for answers to problems?						Let problems defeat you?
Take risks?						Play it safe?
Take action?						Give up?

Self-image

Our self-image flows from our self-esteem. It is how we see ourselves. Are we competent or helpless, shy or friendly, gentle or severe, fast learners or slow learners, dependable or haphazard?

Self-talk

A good way to assess your level of self-esteem is to listen to your 'self-talk', the silent messages you give yourself throughout the day. Try this little exercise:

What do you say to yourself?

When you've just made a mistake in front of your co-workers:

_____

_____

When you're doing something for the first time and you're finding it difficult:

_____

_____

When you've forgotten to do something you've promised to do:

_____

_____

When you walk into a meeting with people you've never met before:

_____

_____

When the boss calls you in and you don't know why:

_____

_____

When you trip walking down the road to the shop:

_____

_____

When you're running late for an important appointment:

_____

_____

When you can't get your cheque book to balance:

_____

_____

When you've done something particularly well:

_____

_____

What you've just written down will give you an idea about the sort of self-talk you usually use; Appendix 4 provides some further information on this.

What are you telling yourself with your self-talk? Are you sending yourself limiting, rejecting, negative messages? Or are you sending yourself empowering, energising, strengthening messages?

Whether you're right or whether you're wrong, you will always believe yourself.

Check your self-talk. Think positively to act positively to get positive results.

We always believe in our self-talk. And this makes it right.

To increase your self-esteem, make sure your self-talk builds you up, not tears you down.

Our self-talk comes true

People who see themselves as reserved, poor communicators, who make a lot of mistakes and have little to offer, will behave in quite different ways from those people who see themselves as outgoing, capable contributors who are good with people.

The way we value ourselves and see ourselves determines everything we do and say.

And they will achieve quite different results.

The way we behave largely determines the results we reap.

The biggest influence on our results is us. If we behave as if we're reserved, poor communicators, and so on, others will oblige us by relating to us in this way. We will have set the tempo for the dance of communication and our low self-image will be reinforced.

This happens with every aspect of our self-image and self-esteem. These aspects of our personalities lead us to behave in certain ways and the way we behave gets us very predictable results.

We are in a loop. A self-fulfilling prophecy.

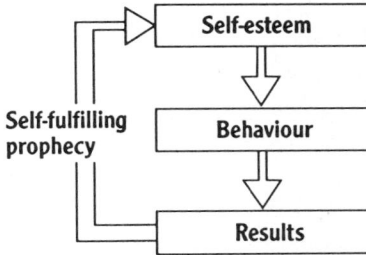

If we don't get the predictable results, we'll ignore those results. If we can't ignore them, we'll reinterpret them and bend them until they fit.

The brain, in its quest for predictability and conformity, will ignore or twist any information that contradicts our self-image (or anything else, such as the mind sets discussed in Chapter 3, that we firmly believe). The friendly overtures made to a shy person will not just be totally overlooked; the brain will not even register them. This is an unconscious and rapid process: 'Musn't let that self-image of shyness crumble', says the unconscious, 'Must make sure that self-talk comes true!'

What does this have to do with body language? Your self-image and self-esteem come across to others before you even speak; in the way you dress; the way you 'carry' yourself; in the amount and type of eye contact you make; the way you sit. This is the way in which self-esteem and self-image set up the communication tempo before the dance even begins.

Raising your self-esteem

Instead of feeling guilty, *see any mistakes you make as valuable lessons.*

Instead of sitting at home, *participate in something you enjoy and develop your talents.*

Instead of over-eating, over-drinking, under-exercising, *take care of yourself.*

Instead of focusing on failures, *focus on your successes.*

Instead of blaming others, *take responsibility for your life; see yourself as the source of what happens to you.*

Instead of hanging out with losers, *hang out with people with high self-esteem.*

Instead of being critical of yourself and others, *look for what is likeable in yourself and in everyone you know and meet.*

Instead of saying 'Oh, it's nothing, really', *say: 'Thank you! Enjoy compliments without embarrassment.*

Much of the content of our self-esteem and self-image is hidden from us in our unconscious. Nevertheless, it controls our behaviour and, through our behaviour, the results we achieve. It stands to reason, then, that the more we understand about ourselves, the more we will be able to take conscious control of the way we behave and respond to events, people, and situations. With high self-esteem and a strong self-image, our options will multiply. We will have more choices in any situation.

Our communication skills will be much improved, too.

Appendix 4
Self-talk as an indicator
of self-esteem

Indicators of low self-esteem	Indicators of high self-esteem
When you've made a mistake in front of your co-workers and you say to yourself:	
'Now they'll *know* I'm useless!'	'Next time, I'll . . .'
When you're doing something for the first time and you're finding it difficult, and say to yourself:	
'I'm so stupid; I can never learn anything!'	'I've learnt things like this this before; I'll get it if I keep at it.'
When you've forgotten to do something you'd promised to do, and say to yourself:	
'I'm so stupid and forgetful!'	'That's not like me. This is how I'll fix this up . . .'

Indicators of low self-esteem	Indicators of high self-esteem

When you walk into a meeting with people you've never met before and say to yourself:

'I hate this; I'm terrible with strangers.'	'This will be a challenge; I'll keep calm and everything will be fine.'

When the boss calls you in and you don't know why, and you say to yourself:

'I'm in for it now; I must have made another mistake again.'	'I wonder what's up.'

When you trip walking down the road to the sandwich bar and say to yourself:

'What a clod I am; I can't even walk down the road without making a fool of myself!'	'Goodness! I'd better pay more attention to where I'm going!'

When you're running late for an important appointment and say to yourself:

'Trust me to be late again. I'm always late. I make a mess of everything.'	'This isn't like me to be late. I'd better get to a telephone to warn them.'

Indicators of low self-esteem	Indicators of high self-esteem
When you can't get your cheque book to balance and say to yourself:	
'I'm hopeless at this kind of stuff. I'll never get it right.'	'This has to be done and I know I can do it.'

When you've done something particularly well and say to yourself:	
'Miracles can happen! That was lucky.'	'I'm really good at this.'

First impressions count!

You have only one chance to make a good first impression.

Rightly or wrongly, first impressions often leave lasting impressions. They can give us a great start or they can betray us for a long time to come.

Image—look the part

Fifty-nine per cent of a first impression is made up of how we look: the way we dress, the jewellery we wear and accessories we carry. Other, less controllable factors, such as age, height, and weight also form part of this.

Let's begin with the symbolic communication of dress. Dress however you want to at home. In business, dress well and follow the unwritten (but real) 'uniform code' of your organisation. This might be fairly casual clothing, sombre suits, or suits with a touch of colour in the shirt or tie, scarf, or necklace. Men normally avoid brown suits and safari suits for business and any fashion extreme is generally avoided by women in business.

If you haven't already done so, take a look at the people around you and formulate some guidelines for yourself. The aim is to look professional without making any fashion statements.

If your career aspirations are upward, you may want to dress the same way as the people at the level above you dress; or dress the way the people in the department or section you want to move into dress. This will make you seem like them and increase your chances of that promotion or transfer.

If you aim to be seen as a capable professional, wear the best quality clothing and accessories your budget allows you. Agreed, these may have little to do with your actual performance or competence, but symbolically, your personal presentation communicates a strong message and affects how you are perceived by others.

Body language—put your best foot forward

Most of the remaining 41 per cent of the first impression we create, and sustain, comes from our body language. The kind of body language most likely to make a favourable and professional first impression and earn us attention and respect includes open hand movements that are relaxed yet 'measured' in pace (not extreme, sudden or 'quick'), an upright posture (not slouching or cowering), and head held up.

Firm eye contact (but not staring them down), a neutral facial expression or one that accurately reflects your inner feelings, and a relaxed (but not loose) jaw are also important.

Smile (unless it is clearly unsuitable). A sincere smile releases endorphines, 'feel-good energy chemicals'; these cannot help but improve the first impression you make as well as the entire communication process.

When appropriate, and particularly when meeting someone for the first time or after a period of not having seen each other, offer to shake hands. The physical contact establishes a cordial atmosphere and sets the scene for a friendly encounter. Increase this by looking genuinely pleased to meet or see them again, and the first impressions will be positive ones.

Voice—ring true!

Your first few words will also set the tone of what follows. Your voice should be steady, calm, and strong, without being overly loud (or quiet). Your words should flow together fluently, without awkward hesitations, in a steady, even pace, emphasising key words and phrases.

Create a positive first impression through your stance, actions, expressions, and personal presentation (dress and accessories).

First impressions count. Make sure yours counts in your favour.

Manage your body language

As we saw in Chapter 20, most people read body language automatically and well, although our conclusions often go straight into our subconscious.

Few of us, however, attend to our own body language. This deprives us of a great deal of potential control over the messages we are sending to others non-verbally and thus over the communication process itself.

Remember the first three Communication Basics?

1. Everything you do is a communication.

2. The way the message is delivered always affects the way the message is received.

3. The real communication is the message *received*, not the message *intended*.

Managing your own body language is important. You want to send compatible messages at all levels, including the non-verbal. The better you manage your body language, the stronger your communications will become.

Here is a mnemonic to help you remember the main aspects of managing your body language:

SO CLEAR

As we go through each element, remember that to some extent, body language is culturally shaped, particularly its more subtle aspects. Where relevant, there is also information on some of the main cultural differences likely to be found in Australia.

S is for the way you sit or stand and the way you use space

Sitting or standing directly opposite someone, or squaring up to them, is subconsciously perceived as confrontational. It puts the communicators into fighting mode.

Sit or stand more at right angles than directly opposite.

This sends co-operative messages and gives both parties more gazing space when looking away to think. Traditional Aboriginal Australians often stand side-by-side at even more than 90 degrees.

As far as you can, try and sit or stand on the same level as the person you're talking to.

Height can be used to place people at a disadvantage, so if you are taller than average, be careful your height doesn't intimidate people. Moving slightly away from other people so they don't have to crane their necks looking up at you can help.

Watch your use of personal space. We each have an invisible personal space zone around us and beware anyone who enters it!

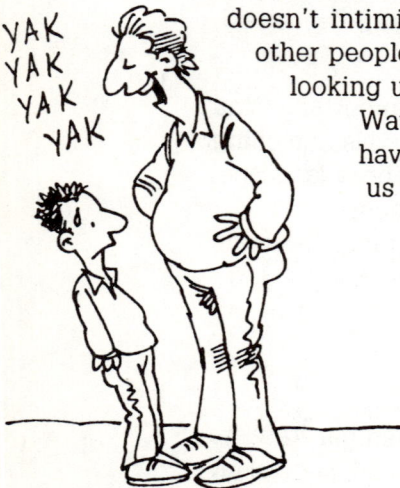

YAK
YAK
YAK
YAK

Stand at arm's length from people in business encounters.

Personal space zones

- close friends or family: up to 45 cm or 18 inches
- friends or close co-workers: 45 to 80 cm or 1.5 to 2.5 feet
- co-workers or acquaintances: 60 to 120 cm or 2 to 4 feet
- strangers (depending on how you   about 150 cm or 5 feet
  perceive their level of friendliness)

There are cultural differences in personal space zones that often have to be taken into account when communicating with people from cultures other than our own. The figures given above apply to most white Australians, although Australians from country areas tend to have larger personal space zones than people from cities. Northern Europeans, North Americans and Asians seem to have a slightly larger personal space zone than white Australians do. Southern Europeans have slightly smaller zones, while people from Middle Eastern cultures have even smaller space zones.

While touching is infrequent in most Australian business situations, it sometimes occurs: someone might pat another person on the back or place a hand on a shoulder, for instance. Asians, however, unless they are very 'westernised', generally do not touch at all.

When communicating with people from a different culture, take cues about personal space zones and physical contact from them.

Sensitivity to such boundaries can save a great deal of embarrassment, discomfort and misunderstanding.

O is for the openness of your expression and movements

In the following cartoon the visual difference between the non-verbal messages each person is sending is quite distinct. The person on the left conveys unspoken messages

WHO WOULD YOU RATHER HAVE
A CONVERSATION WITH ?

about not wanting to hear, being closed to new ideas and information, defensiveness, self-protection, and even fear. Body language like this lets us down by giving a negative impression to others. It also impedes the communication process because it is difficult to give good information to someone sending out such signals.

In contrast, the openness of gestures and body position of the person on the right conveys signals of openness of thoughts, mind, and attitudes; openness to communication and to hearing what others have to say; and even of trustworthiness. It is far easier to give good information to an 'open' person than to a 'closed' person.

C is for how exclusively you centre your attention on the other person

As we discussed in Chapter 16, focusing on, or centring your attention on the speaker markedly improves communication. In particular, it helps the speaker to give good information and improves the listener's ability to hear it.

The more important a communication is, the more important it is to push any other thoughts from your mind and focus wholly on the speaker and on what is being said.

Centre your body, too, by orienting it towards the other person. This also encourages the speaker to continue and reduces the chances that you will be distracted by things going on around you.

In short, make the speaker and the topic at hand the centre of your attention.

L is for how you lean to show attention, apply pressure, or reduce pressure

When listening, we can signal that we are paying close attention to the speaker by leaning slightly towards that person. This communicates interest and involvement in the conversation.

If we lean beyond about 75 degrees, however, attentiveness can become 'pressure'. It can subtly say 'I don't believe you' or 'You'd better come clean' or 'You'd better agree'. It can also invade the other's personal

space. While we may not consciously realise why, we can feel cornered when someone leans too close to us.

The '75 degree to 60 degree lean' has the potential, if sensitively used, to be a subtle and tactful technique for persuasion and for finding out more information. Insensitively used, it can be a bullying, domineering, and manipulating technique that can easily backfire.

Conversely, if you want to reduce pressure, say, because someone is looking nervous, becoming emotional, or talking about difficult personal matters, you can lean slightly back to reduce some of the pressure they might be feeling. Again, there's a fine line, because leaning too far back gives the impression of total disinterest.

E is for the way you make eye contact to reassure the other person and to apply or reduce pressure

In European and European-descent cultures, eye contact is very important. After all, the eyes are considered to be the mirrors of the soul. Parents tell their children: 'Look at me when I'm speaking to you!' and 'Look me in the eye and say that!' Friends say: 'He couldn't even look me in the eye'.

With too little eye contact we become disinterested listeners or untrustworthy speakers; with too much eye contact we become bullies.

The 'right' level of eye contact from a speaker says 'I'm telling you the truth; you can believe what I say'. It also helps hold the listener's attention. The 'right' level of eye contact from a listener says 'I'm interested in you and what you have to say; I'm following you'. It also helps the speaker by showing that they are being listened to.

The difficulty here is that the 'right' level of eye contact often varies between cultures. In some cultures, such as the Australian Aboriginal culture, a level of eye contact that white Australians feel comfortable with is considered disrespectful and an invasion of personal space. In fact, generally speaking, in Aboriginal Australian culture, averting your eyes is a sign of respect.

Many people from Asian cultures are comfortable with lower levels of eye contact than white Australians are, for similar reasons. In fact, when listening, Asians often close their eyes. White Australians might panic at this unless they realise that this indicates a highly concentrated level of listening; it is done to block out all distractions in order to listen intensely to the speaker. It is, in fact, quite a compliment.

Bearing these important cultural differences in mind, slightly increased levels of eye contact (without or staring the other down) can be used to increase pressure in a way that is similar to the '75 degree to 60 degree lean'. Conversely, slightly reduced eye contact can reduce pressure. Sensitivity is again the key.

A is for how appropriately you respond to the speaker

In Chapters 17 and 18 we looked at the skill of active listening and the importance of restating your understanding, to be sure of accurate communication and to help you gather more information. In Chapter 19 we looked at the importance of repeating the gist of what a person has just said before asking another fact-gathering question in order to avoid creating the impression of an 'interrogation'.

This, essentially, is what appropriately responding consists of. It is the opposite of abruptly leading the conversation onto a different tack.

Appropriate responses build on, extend or clarify what the speaker has said. Such responses lend smoothness and a natural rhythm to the flow of a conversation.

R is for how relaxed and balanced you are when communicating

Some people have a habit of constantly jiggling their feet or legs, or tapping their fingers or a pencil. They give an impression of constant nervous movement, or agitation. Others lean at extreme angles when they are sitting or standing. With some, it is their heads only; with others, their torsos.

These habits may not distract *them*, but they can distract other people and hamper communication. They also send non-verbal messages that other people are likely to interpret as 'I'm not interested', 'I'm bored and want to get out of here', 'I'm nervous and uncertain', or 'I'm flustered'. Inner turmoil, inner confusion, or excitement may be perceived from jiggling, tapping or leaning. These may be done purely through habit; even so, they are a distraction.

Stillness and balance, on the other hand, need not imply stiffness. A person can be comfortably still and relaxed. The effect is quite different from that of the constant jiggler, tapper, or leaner. Being relaxed and balanced assists communication.

Purely from habit, most of us do one or two things 'wrong'. While it is better to do them all 'right', you probably don't need to change your habits overnight. This could require quite a concerted effort. However, the more important a communication is to you, the more essential it is that you get each of these key aspects of body language 'right'.

The more we stray from the SO CLEAR ideal described above, the more uncomfortable with us the other person will feel. Communication will suffer accordingly. So any concerted effort you make at checking your body language and correcting any distracting habits will be well rewarded. Eventually, 'doing it all right' will become an unconscious habit; you will do it automatically.

Manage your body language—It's SO CLEAR

S   Sit or stand at right angles and on the same level, and respect people's personal space zones.

O   Use open gestures and body language.

C   Centre your attention exclusively on the other person.

L   Lean slightly forward to show interest; a bit further forward to apply pressure; slightly back to reduce pressure.

E   Maintain appropriate eye contact while listening to encourage the speaker; increase eye contact to apply pressure, and reduce it to lower pressure.

A   Appropriately respond by basing your responses on what the other person has just said.

R   Be relaxed and balanced to make relaxed and open communication easier.

Build rapport through body language

24

When you have rapport with someone, you feel that you are 'in synch', in harmony, on the same wavelength. This creates a sense of affinity and unity. It helps build relationships. It fosters co-operation and teamwork. It helps achieve results.

The next time you are in a restaurant or other public place, watch various pairs of people. Which pairs seem to have a rapport and which ones do not? Why?

When two people, or even a group of people, are in rapport, you will notice that very often the **body language** of one is reflected in the other or others; they will be sitting in a very similar or even identical position, for example, or they will be leaning forward at the same angle or crossing their legs in the same way.

Their *movements* often coincide, too. For example, when one person shifts position, the other does, or when one person reaches for a drink, the other does. Or they might both be swinging their legs to the same, unheard rhythm.

If you look more closely, you might notice more subtle things the pairs have in common. For instance, they both might be *breathing* in unison, or their *voices* might match each other in volume, pitch, or pace. If you could overhear their conversation, you might also notice that they use the same or similar *expressions*, speak with a similar *intensity* in their voices, or make the same *gestures* with the same level of *energy*.

Matching

This is called matching. Matching is something that we all do naturally and unconsciously whenever we are in rapport with someone.

People usually don't consciously notice that they are matching; but their subconscious notices. Subconsciously, they each think: 'This person is really like me in a lot of ways; therefore she or he must be all right'. This reinforces and strengthens their liking for each other.

Build rapport through matching

You can use this knowledge to build rapport with another person. You can match lots of things: a person's beliefs, personal history, vocabulary, style of dress, body language, breathing . . . The list goes on and on.

You can match a person's whole body position, the position of the upper or lower half of their body, or the angle of their head and/or shoulders. You can match these things precisely, or partially, the choice is yours.

You can match their voice: its volume, speed, pitch, rhythm, inflections, intonations and pauses. You can match how rapidly and where they breathe (upper chest, lower chest, or stomach) and how they breathe (shallowly or deeply). You can match their expressions or language style, or some of the phrases and words they use.

Cross-over mirroring

Or you can do what is known as cross-over mirroring. For example, if the person's right leg is crossed over the left leg, you cross your left leg over your right leg; if they are rubbing their right forearm with their left hand, you rub your left forearm with your right hand.

You can match or mirror a person's mannerisms, movements and gestures, and the speed of their movements and gestures. You can match their voice: its volume, speed, pitch, rhythm, inflections, intonations, and pauses.

The idea here is not to copy blindly every movement a person makes or each position they sit in. Rapport is something we do *with* a person, not *to* a person.

Don't use the matching technique if it feels unnatural, uncomfortable, or insincere—this just makes it an empty technique and does nothing to build rapport.

It is important that when you match someone's body language, they do not consciously notice it. *Subtlety is the key.* You don't want them to think: 'Gee, every time I scratch myself, so does he. Every time I move, or sigh, so does he'. Or: 'I wish she'd stop copying me'. Their conscious minds shouldn't notice.

> Use the matching technique only when you sincerely want to build rapport and improve communications between yourself and another person and when you feel true respect for the other person.

PARROT HELL

> *Rapport is gentle. Use the matching technique gently and discreetly.*

Lead to test for rapport

Sometimes it will be important to get a clear idea of the level of rapport between yourself and another person. If you were about to ask an important question or close a sale, for example, you would probably want to do whatever you could to ensure a positive result by asking your question only when you felt certain that sufficient rapport had been built up.

You can test for rapport by a technique known as **leading**. Very simply, you shift your position and see if the other person follows. If the other person follows your lead, matching your new position, this will indicate that you are in rapport. The more positively and quickly you are followed, the deeper your rapport is likely to be.

You don't always have to shift your position: you could talk more quickly or slowly, or more loudly or softly; you could reach for a pen and fiddle with it; you could scratch your shoulder or your ankle; you could take a sip of coffee.

Whatever you do, if you and the person you are with are in rapport, their subconscious will notice that your body language no longer matches and they will shift theirs to bring it into line with yours. When this happens, you can be quite certain that you are 'in synch' and communication is flowing.

Use the leading technique when you feel you are in rapport and you want to confirm it.

The importance of rapport in communication cannot be overemphasised. The more important a communication situation is, the more you may want to think about using the matching technique to build rapport quickly, and the leading technique to test for rapport.

Other people's body language: are you succeeding or missing the mark? 25

As mentioned in Chapter 20, most of us read others' body language intuitively and quickly. Sometimes, however, it can be helpful to look out for particular positive and negative signals. Then we can adjust the way we are sending our message to make the communication process more successful.

At first, you will probably need to check other people's body language consciously; after a while, noticing and adjusting your communication accordingly becomes a habit.

Many body language signals are self-explanatory when you think about them: a tapping foot can indicate we are anxious to be on our way; rubbing our neck can say: 'You give me a pain in the neck'; a quick intake of breath can signal surprise or sudden understanding.

Caution!

We need to be careful how we interpret. Crossed arms *can* say: 'I feel somehow threatened by what you're saying and I'm closed to hearing it'; they can also say: 'I'm cold!' A tapping foot might mean we'd like to be on our way; it might also reflect a lot of nervous energy. Scratching our head may mean puzzlement or uncertainty;

or it may mean that our head itches. So, there are no fixed rules, only general principles. Individual body language signals should be interpreted, not in isolation, but as part of a cluster of signals.

Body language should be interpreted in context.

Observe signal clusters

Most body language signals appear in clusters, or groups. To continue with the crossed arms example, if our crossed arms were accompanied by rubbing our upper arms with our hands and perhaps stomping our feet and hunching up our shoulders, most people would feel fairly safe in concluding that we were cold.

Always think about the context in which the body language occurs and observe clusters of signals, not solitary signals.

If, on the other hand, our crossed arms were accompanied by looking away from the speaker, tapping a foot, and occasionally shaking our head, others could reasonably reach the conclusion that we disagreed with what was being said.

Observe movements

Any movements, particularly sudden movements, can also indicate a person's inner state. A sudden shift in position, for example, can be very telling.

If a person suddenly uncrosses their legs, reorients their body towards you and leans slightly forward, you may well have just said something they strongly approve of, or want to hear more about. If you noticed this, you would probably want to think about what you just said and what in particular might have been received favourably.

Develop the habit of watching people's body language. Try and discover whether anything you might have said or done could have triggered particular reactions. Adjust your communication to lead to the best result possible.

Be on the lookout for negative signals

A person's body language can act as an early warning signal that something is amiss in the communication process. Negative signals include:

- feet pointed away from you
- rapid nodding of head
- rubbing or scratching neck
- limited eye contact
- body oriented away from you
- covering or rubbing ears
- forming a fist, clenching hands
- fidgeting, for example, rapidly tapping a pencil.
- tapping feet
- covering nose
- looking skyward
- covering mouth
- tense posture
- 'dancing' around
- rapidly exhaling breath

If you see any of the negative body language listed above, alone or especially in clusters, watch out! What might you have just said or done that has put the other person offside? How could you explain things differently? How can you help them see your point of view? What action can you take that will put the communication back on track?

Be on the lookout for positive signals

Just as body language can alert us to problems to come, it can also herald success. Positive body language signals include:

- nodding thoughtfully
- body oriented towards you
- feet pointed towards you
- stroking chin
- eye contact, particularly when pupils are dilated (enlarged)

- relaxed posture
- open hands
- thoughtful 'um-hums'
- open body position.
- handling the documents or materials you are presenting

When you notice any of these favourable signals, particularly if they appear in clusters, make sure you maintain the positive momentum. Notice what you have been saying, how you have been saying it, and what you have been doing. Keep communicating in the current vein.

Thoughtful awareness of others' body language will help you gauge whether you are succeeding or missing the mark in your communications. Likewise, your awareness of and reflection on how you present information, your own body language, and how you encourage other people to present their information, will help improve your success in communicating.

PART V

Put it in writing

Writing for clarity and persuasion

Be concise

26

Business writing is a practical skill. You can improve your writing skills by following a few simple yet essential guidelines.

To improve your writing skills, take two or three memos, reports, and letters you have written and compare each of them with the guidelines in the next two chapters. Choose one or two to rewrite, following the guidelines closely.

At all times remember that business people are busy people. They haven't the time to read something over several times before they fully understand it. They want to pick it up, read it, understand it, act on it, and move on to their next task.

If you write in long, complicated sentences and use too many words, long words, obscure words, jargon, or flowery phrases, your writing will be a chore to read. If you have not clearly stated your purpose, if your main points are unclear and don't stand out, if your thoughts are poorly organised and unattractively laid out, you will be making extra work for your reader. This greatly reduces the chances that what you've written will be read, understood, and acted upon.

These, in fact, are the three criteria of effective business writing:

---

1. It must be easy to read.
2. It must be easy understand.
3. It must persuade readers.

Business writing succeeds if you use short words and short sentences.

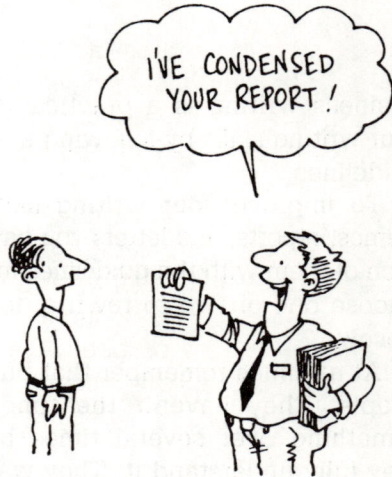

I'VE CONDENSED YOUR REPORT!

Select your words carefully

Use short words

Many people think that long words convey complex ideas and short words convey simple ideas. Their writing is unnecessarily wordy and difficult to read. Certainly, some short words convey simple ideas: 'cat', 'hat', 'sat'. Other short words convey complex ideas: 'truth', 'love', 'soul'. Simple *language*, then, does not necessarily go hand in hand with a simple *subject*. Short words will not make your writing simplistic; they will make it readable.

Choose short words over long words. A word can be considered short if it has less than three syllables. There are three exceptions:

1. Capitalised words ('Australian', 'January', 'Saturday')
2. Combinations of short, easy words ('bookkeeper', 'nevertheless', 'everybody')
3. Words that become three syllables by adding '-es' or '-ed' ('confess<u>es</u>', 'digest<u>ed</u>', 'resourc<u>es</u>').

Note that words ending in '-ing' count as long words if they have three or more syllables. They make writing more difficult to read because they need to be visually processed.

> Use short, familiar words that accurately and precisely convey your meaning.

This is not a hard and fast rule. Some short words are hard: 'thought', 'draught', 'through', 'trough', 'gaol'. Use your judgment. Choose the word that is most precise, economical, and familiar to your readers. These are probably the words you would use when speaking face-to-face.

When to use long words

A lot of long words are used all the time. Some should be used, and others only increase the difficulty of the readers' task.

Use a long word if it is the correct name for something or if it is a technical term (but not jargon). Use a long word only if it is the most *accurate* and says precisely what you want to say; it may be a unique or a particularly descriptive word, for example, or it may add extra meaning.

Use a long word if it saves you using a lot of other, smaller words; for example, the word unemployment is *economical* because it saves us using seven short words: 'the state of being without a job'. Use a long word if it would be more *familiar* to your readers than a shorter word.

Do *not* use a long word because you think it will impress your readers. Most people prefer not to have to look up words in dictionaries when they're busy.

So don't eliminate all long words—only the unnecessary ones. Use the word that best describes what you're saying. Use words that are familiar to your readers. Use words that are economical and rich in connotation.

Some long words	Where short ones would do
accomplish	do
acquiesce	yield, agree
admonition	warning
application	use
approximately	about
circumspect	careful
cognisant	aware
demonstrate	show
determine	find out
fabricate	build
finalise	finish
incorporate	include
is functional	works
modification	change
necessity	need
objective	goal, aim
obligation	duty
provided that	if
subsequently	later, since
substantiate	prove, confirm
sufficient	enough
supersede	replace, update
utilise	use
visualise	picture, see
voluminous	bulky

Avoid jargon and 'buzz words'

For most readers jargon makes writing harder to read. The same is true for currently fashionable 'buzz words': we don't all share the same meaning of them.

If you want to use jargon or 'buzz words', be certain your readers will have exactly the same understanding of them that you do.

Use short sentences

Many people equate bulk with importance. They pad their writing with flowery phrases and transitions, filler words, complicated sentence structures, redundancies, and qualifiers. This does nothing to make their writing easy to read and understand.

Long sentences tire and lose the reader. They stop your message from being read, understood and acted on. Short sentences help break up our thoughts. They help us pick out each point out clearly, and they help readers to grasp each thought readily.

Aim for an average sentence length of 18 words. Include some very short sentences of under ten words.

Short sentences don't make writing simplistic, but they do make it easier to read and understand. They increase the likelihood that your memo, letter or report will be acted on.

Fortunately, long sentences are fairly easy to correct. There are three main ways to shorten sentences: cross out unnecessary words (often found in unnecessary and flowery phrases and redundancies). Take out compound (two-in-one) sentences by removing connectors, and inserting full stops. Reduce sentence complexity by removing qualifying words, such as *however, excepting, provided that* and so on, and making two sentences.

Take out unnecessary phrases

Many unnecessary phrases creep into business writing. They are extra words the reader must plod through. They increase the length of sentences and reading difficulty. Which of the following unnecessary phrases do you recognise?

Unnecessary phrases	Possible substitutions
after this is accomplished	then
assuming that	if
be of assistance	help, assist
come to an end	end, finish
during this time	while
due to that fact that	because, since
except in a very few instances	usually
for the purpose of	for, to
for the reason that	because, since
face up to	face, accept
in order to	to
in the event that	if
in close proximity to	near
in the first place	first
in short supply	scarce, rare
make the acquaintance of	meet
often do not	seldom
on the grounds that	because, since
on account of the fact that	because
render assistance to	help, assist
subsequent to	after
the only difference being	except
the question as to whether or not	whether, if
there are not many who	few
with reference to	about, concerning
within the realm of possibility	possible

Take out redundancies

Redundancies are unnecessary repetitions. They are so
common that we seldom realise they say the same
thing over again without adding anything to the message.
They just add words.

freezing cold	lead pencil
green coloured hat	new addition
live band	total elapsed time
fell down	azure blue
tiny little	total and utter
period of time	time schedule

They add length to sentences and increase reading difficulty.
Challenge your use of phrases, especially often-used
ones. If a word doesn't add meaning, take it out.

- This service is available ~~on an~~ around the clock
  ~~basis~~.
- . . . to see ~~on a~~ first hand ~~basis~~ . . .
- This offer, made only to ~~individually~~ selected executives,
  makes available 70 ~~different~~ products in five ~~different~~
  states and is valid for six ~~full~~ months.
- ~~The purpose of~~ this letter is to ~~provide an~~ ~~explanation
  of~~ (explain) how we reached our decision.
- ~~At the present time,~~ there are (now) . . .
- This generates ~~a~~ monthly ~~quantity of~~ business ~~to
  the value of~~ (worth) . . .
- These interviews should be supportive ~~in nature.~~
- Inventory ~~stock~~
- We are ~~currently~~ investigating . . .
- Expand ~~our business into areas~~ beyond . . .
- ~~Current~~ procedures require . . .
- . . . ~~necessary~~ action required.

Separate compound sentences

We often make two sentences out of one when really a sentence should convey one thought and only one thought and it should have one subject and one verb. *OOPS!*.

We often make two sentences out of one. A sentence should convey only one thought. It should have one subject and one verb. *That's better.*

Try to remove words such as 'and', which are often used to make two sentences one. Insert a full stop in their place.

Reduce sentence complexity

Reduce sentence complexity which will make your writing much easier to grasp and therefore help it be more effective. *OOPS.*

Reduce sentence complexity, to make your writing easier to grasp. *That's better.*

Don't ramble

There is a difference between legitimate qualifiers and longwinded, rambling thoughts. The latter occur because our fast-working brain keeps feeding in thoughts as we write. Before we know it, we've written a really long, complex, rambling sentence.

You're writing: *'We have experienced this problem for some time'*. This is a sentence. While you're writing it, though, your brain keeps thinking and feeds more information in which you add to the sentence: *'which we have discussed on a number of occasions and which we have, unfortunately, tried to no avail to rectify but what we could try now, I'd like to suggest, is . . .'*

Try to remove words such as 'because', 'therefore', 'however', and 'thus'. Insert a full stop and make each sentence stand alone.

HE TRIED TO READ OUT HIS RAMBLING ENTRY, COULDN'T FIND THE TIME TO TAKE A BREATH AND FAINTED!

Include some very short sentences—one to ten words

This will really cut down your average sentence length and help make your writing readable. It will add bounce and energy to your writing and make it interesting and persuasive.

You cannot control the complexity of your subject matter, but you *can* control the complexity with which you write about it. You can choose how concise and readable your writing is: choose short words and short sentences. This can make a complex subject easier to understand.

Make your writing persuasive and easy to understand

27

Do whatever you can to make it easier for your readers to understand your message and take action on it. This chapter looks at some more ways to make your writing readable and at how you can write persuasively.

Grammar

Grammar is important. In fact, one definition of business writing is: *'Conversation with cleaned-up grammar'*. Readers often judge our message by how grammatically it is presented.

If you're concerned about your grammar, you could start a campaign to improve it. Study a good book on English grammar. Listen to friends, co-workers, television and radio presenters who speak well. Note how they construct their sentences and how they use verbs. Read good books.

Until you become confident, ask someone to check over your letters, reports, and memos for you.

Organise your material

Use a spidergram

A spidergram is a simple yet incredibly useful technique for organising and sequencing information and ideas. It will also help prevent omissions, redundancies, and irrelevancies, and highlight what information should be added.

To make a spidergram, **Step 1:** put your theme or topic in the centre of the page and draw a circle around it. **Step 2:** note your purpose. Without a clear purpose to work towards, it will be nearly impossible to write anything clearly. Some common purposes in business writing are:

to analyse	to interpret	to explain
to discuss	to propose	to present
to request	to recommend	to review
to thank	to confirm	to outline

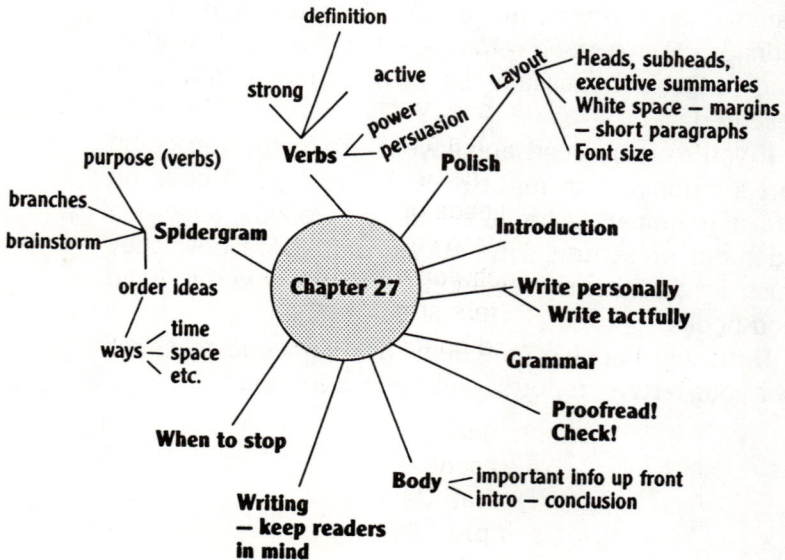

definition

strong   active

power

persuasion

Verbs

purpose (verbs)

branches

brainstorm — **Spidergram**

order ideas

time

ways — space

etc.

When to stop

Writing
— keep readers
in mind

Chapter 27

Layout — Heads, subheads,
executive summaries
White space — margins
— short paragraphs
Font size

Polish

Introduction

Write personally
Write tactfully

Grammar

Proofread!
Check!

Body — important info up front
intro — conclusion

If you know what your purpose is, you will be able to sequence your information and ideas to meet it. If you have more than one purpose, that's fine.

If you are writing a report that will have several long sections, consider making a spidergram for each section. Each section has a different purpose.

Step 3: brainstorm all the information you could include.

If relevant use a verb plus a noun. Verbs denote action; they remind you what to do. For example, *ask questions* is more clear than *questions*.

If several thoughts seem to attach themselves to one main idea, include them as 'branches'.

Step 4: take a look at your spidergram. Do you want to include everything on it? Cross out anything that is unnecessary or repetitive.

Step 5: what information or data do you need to gather, check, or develop? Highlight these.

Does anything else to include occur to you? Add it now.

> Make your business writing as CONCISE as possible. The shorter the better. Remember the KISS principle: Keep it Short and Simple!

Order your ideas

How should you sequence your ideas? Once your spidergram is constructed, it's a simple matter of ordering the information in a way that seems logical to you and most appropriate to the needs of your readers.

Step 6: attach a number to each arm of the spidergram to show the order in which you want to present it.

Plan to lead your readers step by step through your thoughts, information, and conclusions. There are many ways to do this:

Time	Chronological
	Past → Present → Future
Space	Geographical: Central point → outwards; for example, Sydney → suburbs, or Melbourne docks → all over Australia

definition

(7c) active

(7b) strong

power persuasion (7a)

Layout — Heads, subheads, executive summaries
White space — margins — short paragraphs
Font size

Verbs

(3a) purpose (verbs)

(3c) branches

(3d) brainstorm

(3) Spidergram

(7)

Polish (8)

(1) Introduction

Write personally
(9) Write tactfully

Chapter 27

(3e) order ideas

(3b) ways — time / space / etc.

Grammar (2)

Proofread!
(10) Check!

When to stop (4)

(5)

(6) Body — important info up front
intro — conclusion

Writing — keep readers in mind

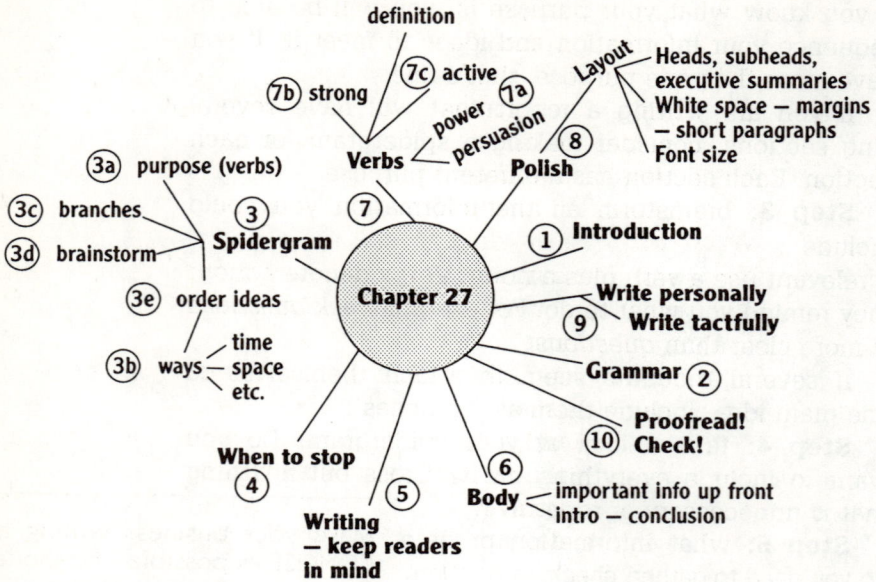

Causal Process	Facts → Cause(s) → Effect: Sequential steps: for example, raw material → manufacturing stages → product
Principle	theory → practice; for example, write readably → short words, short sentences, avoid jargon, take out unnecessary phrases, redundancies, compound sentences, reduce sentence complexity, include some very short sentences
Problem	Possible solutions; for example, overweight → go on a diet, exercise more, visit a health farm, buy larger clothes, wire jaws together
Comparison and contrast	for example, acting and miming, sketching, and painting, efficient versus effective, urgent versus important

Order   descending order: larger to smaller, or
                      ascending order: smaller to larger

Recommendation
                      Facts→ Conclusion→ Recommendation: for
                      readers who like details.
                      Conclusions→ Recommendations→ Facts
                      or Reasons: for readers who may prefer
                      to overlook the details.
                      Recommendations→ Conclusions→ Facts:
                      for readers who know the background
                      and who trust your thinking.
                      Conclusions→ Facts→ Recommendations:
                      this is unusual. It catches the readers'
                      attention and sets out the logic before
                      presenting the recommendations. It's good
                      for occasions when you think your
                      recommendations might be unpalatable
                      to readers.
                      Benefits→ Idea or Recommendation→
                      Rationale: to persuade readers.

Which works best? They're all useful. Build up your
ideas in a way that will communicate them clearly and
persuasively.

How much is enough?

What is the purpose of your letter, report, or memo?
When you have included the necessary information to
meet your objective, it is time to stop.

Include *everything* that is *necessary*
and *only* what is necessary. This
helps make your writing concise.

Some self-check questions

- Should I include the benefits as well as the features?
  (*the sizzle as well as the sausage*)
- Should I include the rationale behind my proposal?
- Is any information redundant or unnecessary to my purpose?
- Have I included everything important to my purpose?
- Will this meet my reader's needs?
- Do I need more, or less, depth of coverage?

Now go and gather any information you will need.

Write it!

You now have a clear purpose to work toward; you know what to include and in what order; and you have gathered any information you need. It's time to begin writing it.

Keep your readers in mind

Identify your readers as closely as you can. Choose your words, supporting information, and organisation of material to suit the readers and your message.

Here are some questions to consider:

- How much background information do your readers already have and how much will you need to supply?
- How well do your readers understand the subject?
- What are your readers' opinions about the subject?
- What are your readers' opinions about you?

- What is your relationship to the readers?
- What are your readers' preferred communication styles? Are they formal or informal?
- What information technique is most likely to achieve your aims? Decide whether it is highly technical, statistical, a general overview or anecdotal; whether it involves cost figures, examples, personal stories or references; how your proposal ties in with corporate policy, and so on. (See also Chapter 15.)

The body

The outline you developed from your spidergram will form the body of your report, memo, or letter.

Put your important information up-front

There are two ways you can put important information up-front. We've talked about using short words and short sentences. Use short paragraphs, too.

The eye is drawn to the beginning of paragraphs. This is where you want to put your important information. Short paragraphs give you more 'up-front' positions to make your points.

The second way to put important information up-front is to put it in the main part of your sentences. This is usually near the beginning of sentences, not following such words as 'when', 'after', 'while', because', 'however', 'therefore', or 'if'.

Write in short paragraphs to break up the writing visually and to give you more 'upfront' places to put important information.

Write an introduction and conclusion

Now go back and write an introduction and a conclusion.

TELL THEM :
- BEFORE
- DURING
- AFTER

INTRODUCTION:

Tell them what you're going to tell them

BODY:

Tell them

CONCLUSION:

Tell them what you've told them

The introduction serves two purposes.

It helps capture interest and indicates what readers should *know* or *do* after reading your memo, letter, or report.

The *introduction* helps your readers. It tells them immediately what they are reading and what the point of it is. This helps them to know what to look for when reading your report, memo, or letter. It also helps them decide what action to take after reading it. The *conclusion* summarises or confirms this.

Even short memos and letters benefit from introductions and conclusions, even if these are only one or two sentences long.

Write your introduction clearly. Outline your topic in one or two sentences. Then state your purpose or the action you hope the readers will take after reading your report, letter, or memo.

Restate your main points and, if appropriate, point to the next steps in your conclusion.

Write persuasively

Persuasive writing is important in business. After all, we don't write business letters, reports, or memos just for fun. We write them because we want somebody to know, understand, or, do something as a result of our written communication.

The power of writing is in the verbs. Write using strong verbs in an active voice. This helps your writing to persuade your readers of your argument.

Use strong verbs

Strong verbs form a clear picture in people's minds. They make your writing powerful and persuasive because they direct thoughts in readers' minds. Writing is more concise and interesting to read if you use strong verbs.

Choose verbs that specifically describe an action.

Strong verbs are **specific** and to do with **action**. Weak verbs are usually a form of the verb *to be*: *am, are, was, were, been, being, be,* and so on.

Weak	Strong
We went to visit . . .	We visited . . .
I am strongly in support . . .	I strongly support . . .
We are able to recommend . . .	We recommend . . .
I will send you . . .	I will fax you . . .
I will go there and . . .	I will drive there and . . .
We will contact you . . .	We will telephone you . . .

Use lots of strong, specific verbs that form a mental picture.

Use active verbs

Make your writing more persuasive by writing actively, not passively. This refers to the relationship between the actor and the action, or verb.

An active sentence puts **the actor** in front (to the left) of the **action,** or verb.

Passive	Active
It was decided by the committee that . . .	The committee decided that . . .
The investigation was carried out by us . . .	We investigated . . .
Inquiries have been made . . .	We asked . . .
Our strategy has been formulated . . .	We have formulated our strategy . . .
It is with sincere regret . . .	I sincerely regret . . .
Your thoughts are appreciated . . .	We appreciate your thoughts . . .
It was agreed that . . .	We agreed that . . .

Polish your writing to meet the reader's needs

Make your writing look inviting to read

Have you ever picked up a report, memo, letter, or magazine article that was one big blur of words? If you have, you will probably also recall the sinking 'Oh no!' feeling that went along with it. 'Do I really have to read this?' is most people's reaction to writing that looks like a sea of uninterrupted words with little white space and long paragraphs.

Keep your paragraphs short. Leave plenty of spaces between them. Make your margins (side, top, and bottom) wide. As far as practical, use large print (12 point font size or above).

You can avoid an 'Oh no!' response from your readers by choosing short words, short sentences, and short paragraphs. You can also lay out what you have written in a way that is appealing to the eye.

White space is the key. It eases the readers' eyes.

Setting out your material like this won't take long and it will make your writing more inviting to read.

Use headings and subheadings

Headings add white space, alert readers to what is to come, and help them to find what they are looking for.

Use executive summaries

These are very useful tools and are included in many business documents. Even a one-page memo can have an executive summary. It takes the form of a well-written, explanatory title which informs readers, just by reading it, what the memo is about.

Long memos and reports can have a full-page executive summary describing the contents or giving information highlights and main conclusions. Readers know when they should read it, how carefully they should read it, and even *if* they should read it.

Write personally

Use 'I', 'you', 'we' when appropriate. Personal pronouns help readers to relate to your writing, making it more direct, clear, and persuasive. They personalise your writing and help make it more readable. They help prevent concise writing from seeming abrupt.

The wheels of organisations are turned by people. Business writing is written by people for other people to read. So don't worry about referring to people in your business writing.

Think of business writing as spoken Englsih with cleaned-up grammar. Write *to* your readers in a personal tone.

Write tactfully

Business writing should not contain judgmental terminology. Report the facts in a professional way and readers can draw their own conclusions. If you want to give an opinion, label it as such—don't masquerade it as a fact.

Consider timing, too. Put yourself in the readers' place before you fire off a memo or letter. Consider matters from their position.

Don't forget to check

Check everything you have written carefully: read and re-read it aloud to yourself, listening to make sure the grammar sounds right, and your meaning is clear.

Then read it aloud again to yourself: does it make sense? Will your readers understand it? Is all the information you need there? Is there anything extra you could cut out? Time spent checking is time very well spent. It will help ensure that what you have written will be easily read, understood and acted upon.

Further reading

Bolton, Robert. *People Skills*, Brookvale: Simon & Schuster Australia, 1987.

This is a good overview of communication.

Covey, Stephen R. *Seven Habits of Highly Effective People*, New York: Simon & Schuster Fireside Books, 1989.

A really terrific book which covers a multitude of skills.

Gordon, Dr Thomas. *Leader Effectiveness Training*, New York: Bantam Books, 1980.

There are several editions of this book under different publishers. All are good. Leader Effectiveness Training contains some of the earliest and most clearly explained techniques for communicating well with others.

Fisher, Roger & Ury, W. *Getting to Yes*, London: Hutchinson Better Business Guides, 1981.

This book looks at how to communicate on a win-win basis, particularly in negotiation situations.

Laborde, Genie Z. *Influencing with Integrity*, Palo Alto, California: Syntony Publishing, 1984.

A lovely and inspiring book.

Myers, Isabel. *Gifts Differing*, Palo Alto, California: Consulting Psychologists Press, Inc., 1986.

Provides a clear description of the 16 Myers-Briggs personality types.

Index